Stock Strategies Success Through Machine Learning.

MICHAEL D. PARKER

Abstract

In 2023 about 61% of adults in the United States invested money in the stock market. The goal of stock market trading, done by both large institutions and individuals, is of course to make a profit. However, many day traders and individual investors fail when it comes to making a good return. Many trades are influenced by psychology and emotion rather than data, which can be analyzed to determine the best stocks to buy at any given time. Algorithmic trading can be used to solve some of these obstacles for individual investors. Algorithmic trading involves setting up rules that cause trades to be automatically executed when specific criteria are met. Some trading strategies can be profitable and many depend on timing and historical data. In this thesis the goal is to predict the best trading strategies for stocks over a given period of time. Furthermore the goal is to predict the best trading strategy to buy and sell a stock during each hour of the trading day. It was possible to predict whether or not trading strategies would be profitable at each hour of the trading day with 69.93% accuracy, beating a baseline value of 50%. It was possible to predict the best strategy overall per hour of the trading day with 29.54% accuracy, beating a baseline value of 11.11%.

Contents

introduction

Stock trading is the buying and selling of shares of publicly traded companies in the stock market, usually through a stock exchange [1]. Many people use stock trading as a means to invest their money and make a profit. While hedge funds are known for trading money on a large scale, there are many people who trade stocks individually [2].

A large part of decision making when it comes to individual traders buying and selling stocks is psychological [3]. When individuals trade in the stock market their decisions are often made emotionally and potentially uninformed [3]. People buy and sell stocks based on non standardized information such as company recognition, past events, current feelings about a company or a one time current event. Traders have a "tendency to make judgments about the likelihood of events based on their recent experience" [3]. The field of "behavioral finance" focuses on "understanding the affect of investors' psychology in their trading strategy and on the market" [4]. This approach fails to consider all of the available data and can result in loss of money. Although stock trading can directly affect a person's livelihood, people tend to go about it emotionally rather than practically in a data-driven way. With this lack of data individual trading can be seen as random purchases and sales of stock.

Day trading is when an individual buys and sells stock within one day [5]. Day traders buy and sell stock frequently throughout the day and usually own the same amount of stock at beginning and end of the day [5]. Less than 20% of day traders make money and even fewer day traders make money consistently [5]. Overall, day traders do not make a significant amount of money [5].

One of the biggest mistakes that investors make is the timing of when they buy and sell stock [6]. One solution to this problem is algorithmic trading. Algorithmic trading is a method of trading stocks based on a set of predefined rules [7]. It has been around since the 1980s but gained popularity starting in 1998 when algorithmic trading became authorized by the U.S Securities and Exchange Commission [8]. Algorithmic trading uses a set of instructions to execute trades based on "timing, price, quantity, or any mathematical model" [7]. In contrast to manual trading, algorithmic trading exclusively uses data to make trading decisions, aiding people in executing trades more efficiently and accurately. Algorithmic trading can be more beneficial than manual trading due to the accuracy, timing, testing abilities, and higher trading volumes which are possible with algorithmic trading. A trade can be executed essentially instantaneously when specific criteria are met. When employing algorithmic trading strategies many financial values are analyzed. Some "[v]ariables such as earnings yield, cash flow yield, book-to-market ratio, and size are shown to have some power predicting stock returns" [9]. Algorithmic trading is used by individual traders as well as large institutions including hedge funds [8]. Hedge funds make a lot of money executing trades but often keep their algorithms proprietary not to be accessed by the general public [10]. Individual traders are at a disadvantage in this regard.

The motivation for this thesis is the desire to minimize the apparent difficulty for individual stock traders to make a profit. We will look at stock data and trading strategies to find patterns and to use machine learning to predict the success of these strategies. More specifically, the goals of this thesis include evaluating multiple trading algorithms and predicting their success over 6 month time periods as well as their success at each hour of the trading day over the same time periods. In this way, there is the hope of making stock trading more accessible and profitable to individuals.

1   Related Work

Studies have been done and papers have been written presenting many different strategies that can be used for trading stocks. Some of these studies describe methods used to predict information about stocks and stock prices. Machine learning (ML) is among some of the methods used for predicting stock trends and patterns.

In a paper written by Napate et al., trading strategies that utilize the simple moving average (SMA) and exponential weighted moving average (EWMA) are described. Both of these strategies compute average prices over a look-back period and compare stock prices to those averages. Crossover methods are also described where different length SMA and EWMA averages are computed and compared to one another. While these strategies are simple, they can be combined with other indicators and used in different ways to create trading rules. These strategies can be beneficial for investors [7].

In a study done by Kumar and Thenmozhi, machine learning models were used to predict the direction (positive or negative) of a stock rather than predicting the actual price of a stock. Random Forest and Support Vector Machine (SVM) machine learning classifiers were used to predict the direction of stock price on a daily level. The SVM model was able to predict with 68.44% accuracy if the day's stock price would increase or decrease from the previous day. The random forest model was able to make the predictions with 67.4% accuracy. These values show that the models were able to make better than random (50%) predictions [9].

In a study done by Wu et al., a filter rule and decision tree algorithm were combined to create a trading strategy. The filter rule used was to buy a stock when the n-day moving average moved up k% from its local low point and was deemed "effective" and to sell when the stock moved down k% from its local high point.

Buying points were considered effective buying points based on values of "money supply, inflation rate, the billings (or revenues) of the upper stream entities in the industry of interest and the price of stock index futures" related to each buying point [11]. The trading points that resulted from this filter rule were then clustered into favorable and unfavorable trading points based on how profitable these points were. A decision tree classifier was used to predict if each point was considered favorable or unfavorable for buying. The strategy's performance was scored on averaged compound annual rate of return (ACARR) which reached a value of 13.26%. In contrast the ACARR value for the filter rule alone was 1.24% [11]. This study shows that using typical algorithmic trading strategies can be improved by using a decision tree algorithm to better predict the profitability of a trading point.

In a study done by Lv et al. six machine learning models and six deep neural networks (DNNs) were compared for their ability to predict the direction of stock prices. The feature set included financial indicators and the targets were the direction of price change from the previous day. The machine learning algorithms performed better than the DNN algorithms predicting direction of returns. The best ML model performed at about 66% accuracy while the best neural network performed at about 52% accuracy [12].

As seen in the papers mentioned in this section, much of the research related to algorithmic trading attempts to predict stock price, returns, direction of stock price and effective trading times. While there are many different algorithms that exist it is difficult to accurately predict stock prices and market trends. Some trading algorithms may work in some scenarios but not in others. They may do well for some stocks but not others.

The work done in this thesis attempts to predict the success of specific trading strategies over a given time period and throughout the day. Many studies only use daily close prices of a stock rather than looking at the data throughout a day. Here, we use stock data throughout the trading day to capture trends based on hour of the day.

We seek to understand the data patterns of the stock market throughout a given day over 6 month time periods. We will show how the time of day during which stocks are traded can impact profits on a daily basis. Furthermore, we will show how different trading strategies can be more successful at different times of the day.

2   Background

2.1 Machine Learning

Machine learning (ML) is a field within computer science in which algorithms are used in order to learn information about a dataset and make predictions about new unseen data [13]. Machine learning models learn relationships between features and labels and make predictions with a degree of accuracy.

2.1.1 Supervised Learning

Supervised learning is when the target labels are known to the model in the training data. The dataset has ground truth values from which the relationships are derived. Model scores are computed by comparing predictions to the true labels.

2.1.2 Regression vs. Classification

Regression and classification are both subsets of supervised machine learning. Regression is when the labels are continuous values and the model computes the predicted values based on a learned curve or function. Classification is when the target labels are a predefined set of classes and predictions are made as to which class each data point belongs. Binary classification is when there are exactly two possible labels and data is categorized into one or the other. We do not use regression here but we use with both binary and multi label classification. Four machine learning models were used for classification. These models are logistic regression (LR), random forest (RF), extreme gradient boosting (XGB) and support vector machine (SVM).

2.1.3 Logistic Regression

Logistic regression is a model used to classify data into groups. It describes the relationship between input features and n possible output classes.

Equation 1 below is used in logistic regression to predict the probability that each data point x belongs to the positive class (1) in binary classification [14].

$$P(x_i) = P(y_i = 1 : x_i) = \frac{1}{1 + e^{X^T \beta}} \tag{1}$$

where

$$X^T \beta = \beta_0 + \beta_1 x_1 + \dots + \beta_n x_n \tag{2}$$

The variables $x_1, x_2, \dots, x_n$ represent independent variables for n number of features and $\beta_0, \beta_1, \dots, \beta_n$ are the coefficients or feature weights.

Logistic regression is a useful model for analyzing stock market data as it is quick to compute and is good for comparison to other models. The solver algorithm and penalty term can be optimized for best results during implementation of this model.

2.1.4 Random Forest Classifier

A random forest classifier is an ensemble method that combines multiple decision trees to predict the class of data points. Each decision tree makes predictions based on a random subset of the data. These independent trees are averaged at the end for optimal results. The tree algorithm seeks to minimize the impurity in the data during each node split or decision made. The Gini impurity is the function we used for our implementation. Equation 3 shows the Gini function [15].

$$g(N) = \sum_{i=j} P(\omega_i)P(\omega_j) \tag{3}$$

where $P(\omega_i)$ is the proportion of data at the given node that belongs to class i [15].

Some of the parameters for random forest implementation that can be optimized include number of trees to use in the ensemble, number of features to use for each prediction and number of samples at each leaf after the maximum decisions are made.

2.1.5 Extreme Gradient Boosting

Extreme gradient boosting is also an ensemble method that uses a tree algorithm, however instead of averaging the results of independent trees, in XGB each tree builds on the previous one improving results with every step [16]. Each subsequent tree attempts to correct the errors made by the previous trees. This model has been used successfully for predicting stock market trends [17].

2.1.6 Support Vector Machine

Support vector classifiers are a subset of SVMs that classify data into categories based on a kernel function. The kernel is an algorithm selected to do the classification.

2.1.7 Grid Search

A grid search is a method of tuning the hyperparameters of a ML model. Multiple values to test are selected for each hyperparameter of a model. A grid search is done by trying all permutations of parameters, selecting one per category at a time. The combination of parameters that produce the best model score on the training data are used for training the model going forward. Each model has its own set of parameters based on its underlying algorithm.

2.1.8 Feature Importance

Feature importance is used to show which features in the training data contribute most to the model and results. The method of feature importance used here is permutation based feature importance. Feature importance based on feature permutation can be used for most models including tree algorithms. Permutation feature importance takes a fitted model and a dataset as input. The algorithm loops through each feature column and shuffles the data in that column only. Predictions are made using the model that was trained with an intentionally disrupted dataset. The model is scored. When the accuracy of predictions goes down it shows that the column which was shuffled is an important feature. If a feature column is shuffled and it has no effect on the accuracy of predictions it shows that the feature is not important to the model. Importance values are assigned to each feature. The importance i of a feature j is defined in equation 4 [18].

$$i_j = s - \frac{1}{K} \sum_{k=1}^{K} s_{k,j}$$

$$(4)$$

where s is the overall model score, $s_{k,j}$ is the model score on the corrupted data and K is the number of repetitions of feature shuffling for the given feature.

2.1.9 One hot encoding

One hot encoding is a method of feature engineering that is used to convert string and categorical data to numerical values that can be used to train a machine learning model. In this method each value in a list becomes its own column and the value in each of those columns is a binary value representing whether or not the data point has that value for that feature.

2.2 Stock Market Background

There are many principles, trading strategies and financial indicators that are used for stock market data analysis and algorithmic trading. Some of the principles we used will be described in this section. Four specific indicators that are used for the trading strategies will also be described in this section.

2.2.1 Trading Principles

When looking for trends in stock market data there are principles and theories that help determine when it might be profitable to buy and sell shares of stock.

A momentum indicator measures change in price and can help show the direction in which the price of a stock is moving [19]. The theory that one value surpassing another indicates positive momentum in stock price and the same value falling below another value indicates negative momentum in stock price is used in some of the trading strategies that will be discussed.

Another theory used for determining when to buy and sell stock is looking at overbought and oversold signals. When a specified value rises above a threshold, the stock can be considered overbought or overvalued, indicating that it is a good time to sell [20]. Conversely, when the same value falls below a lower threshold, the stock can be considered oversold or undervalued, indicating that it is a good time to buy [20]. This principle is also used in some trading strategies that will be discussed.

2.2.2 Rate of return

One method for determining how well a trading strategy performed is to look at rate of return [11]. Equation 5 [11] shows how compound rate of return, R_i, was computed, where $N(i)$ is equal to the number of trading points in the given time period.

$$R_i = \prod_{t=1}^{N(i)} (1 + r_{it}) - 1 \tag{5}$$

where r_i represents the rate of return for buying point i, computed by equation 6.

$$r_i = \frac{s_i * (1 - h - o) - b_i * (1 + h)}{b_i * (1 + h)} \tag{6}$$

In equation 6, h is the commission fee per trade and o is the tax per trade when selling. Without considering these values, a simplified equation for computing returns per buying point can be seen in equation 7.

$$r_i = \frac{s_i - b_i}{b_i} \tag{7}$$

where b_i is the buy price and s_i is the sell price.

2.2.3 Trading Strategies

The four financial indicators that were computed as part of the trading rules are the simple moving average (SMA), slow stochastic oscillator, z-score (for mean reversion strategy) and relative strength index (RSI).

Simple Moving Average An N-day simple moving average is a running average of stock prices looking back over N days from a specified current day. This is a calculation often used in stock market trading and can be utilized for multiple trading strategies. We used the SMA computation as a momentum indicator for the SMA crossover trading strategy. In this strategy a short term moving average is compared to a long term moving average. The strategy creates a buy signal when the short term average crosses over above the long term average indicating that the price is moving upwards and therefore is a good time to buy. A sell signal is created when the short term averages crosses over below the long term average indicating that prices will continue to drop and is a good time to sell [21]. Equation 8 shows the computation for the moving average [22].

$$SMA(n) = \frac{A_1 + A_2 + ... + A_n}{n} \tag{8}$$

where A is the price of the stock at a given period and n is the total number of periods.

Slow Stochastic Oscillator A slow stochastic oscillator is a momentum indicator based on a signal that oscillates between 0 and 100. In this strategy %K line and %D lines are computed using the high and low values of a stock over 2 time periods. These lines form slow and fast moving oscillator lines which when compared form buy and sell signals. The %K line uses the high and low values over a longer time period (typically 14 days) to compute the oscillator values. The %D line is the 3-day SMA of the %K line. Equation 9 shows this formula [23].

$$\%K = 100 * \frac{closeprice - lowestlow}{highesthigh - lowestlow} \tag{9}$$

A buy signal is generated when the %K line falls below the low threshold (typically 20) or when %K rises above the %D line. A sell signal is generated when the %K line rises above the high threshold (typically 80) or when %K falls below the %D line. When the %K line crosses above the high threshold it indicates that the price will reverse direction soon and therefore should be sold.

Similarly, when the %K line crosses below the low threshold it indicates that the price will go up and therefore should be bought. When the %K line crosses a threshold boundary it indicates that there was too much momentum in one direction and therefore a trade is executed. When comparing the %K and %D lines, the %D line is a delayed version of the %K line and can be viewed in a similar way to the SMA crossover strategy. When the %K line rises above %D it indicates that the price will continue to rise and when the %K line falls below the %D line it indicates that the price will continue to fall [23].

When comparing %K and %D lines, the slow stochastic oscillator is being used as a momentum indicator. When comparing the %K line to threshold values, the slow stochastic oscillator is being interpreted based on the overbought and oversold stock theory.

Mean Reversion The mean reversion trading strategy is based on the theory that stock prices will always return to their mean price. The standard deviation of stock prices for a rolling period is used to compute z-score over the time period. Equation 10 shows the z-score formula.

$$Z = \frac{x - \mu}{\sigma}$$

(10)

where x is the stock price, μ is the mean price over the entire time period and σ is the standard deviation of stock price over the time period. The mean and standard deviation for the z-score in the trading strategy are computed as rolling values over n days prior to each data point. A buy signal is generated when the z-score falls below a low threshold (typically -1.5) and sell signal is generated when the z-score rises above a high threshold (typically 1.5) [24].

Relative Strength Index Relative strength index is a financial indicator that measures the change in price over a period of time. It is a momentum indicator and measures the change in stock price in terms of speed. The RSI has values between 0 and 100, similar to the slow stochastic oscillator.

Equation 11 shows the RSI formula [25].

$$RSI = 100 - 100 * \frac{1}{1 + RS} \tag{11}$$

where $RS = \dfrac{average\_gain}{average\_loss}$ over a rolling period of time.

When the RSI value falls below a low threshold (typically 30) it indicates oversold stock and a buy signal is generated. When the RSI value rises above a high threshold (typically 70) it indicates overbought stock and a sell signal is generated [25].

3 Data Exploration

Stock data from 2022 was explored and analyzed for four example stocks in order to get a visual overview of the data before further analysis. The goal of this section is to see if there are any patterns that emerge over a year and within each trading day through stocks Airbnb Inc (ABNB), CVS Health Corp (CVS), Microsoft Corp (MSFT) and JPMorgan Chase & Co (JPM). These stocks represent a variety from two different stock exchanges and 4 different industries. ABNB and MSFT are traded in NASDAQ, while CVS and JPM are traded in the New York Stock Exchange (NYSE). ABNB is in the travel services industry, MSFT is in the "software - infrastructure" industry, CVS is in healthcare plans and JPM is in the "banks - diversified" industry.

3.1 Raw Data

Raw data was plotted for each of the four stocks over 2022. The plots in figure 1 below create a visual representation of some of the data with which we will be working. As expected, the raw data appears to be a random signal. It is difficult to visually decipher patterns. These plots show some examples of how price fluctuates over a year and allow comparison between the prices of the four stocks. An overall downward trend for the year can be seen for ABNB, CVS, MSFT and

JPM. Upward and downward trends can be seen at different points throughout the year.

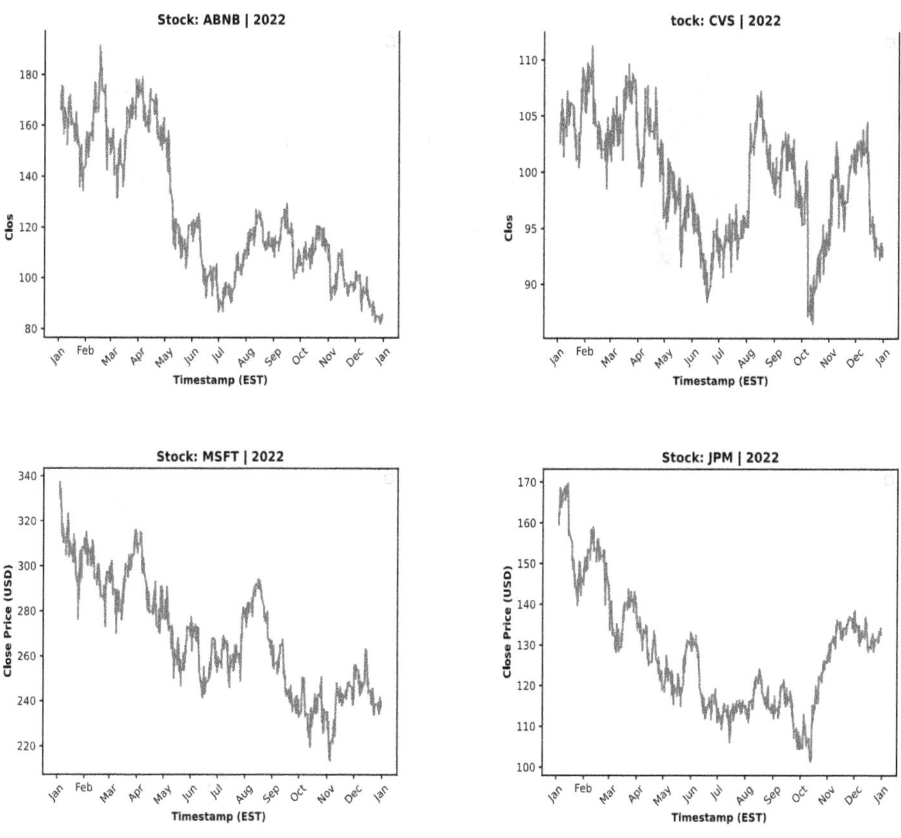

Figure 1: 2022 stock prices for ABNB, CVS, MSFT and JPM

3.2   Hourly Mean Prices

The raw data was aggregated by hour over the entire year. The stock prices were averaged per hour and plotted in figure 2 below. Each data point represents the average price for an hour starting at the time on the x axis. For example, the data point at 9am represents the mean price between 9 and 10am. The data point at 3pm represents the mean price between 3 and 4pm. The average price seems to be higher at the beginning and end of the trading day for ABNB and MSFT. The price remains almost exactly the same over every hour for CVS. The average stock price goes down throughout the trading day. These plots show that the average price per hour can differ for each stock but that there may be peaks and troughs that can be predicted based on the stock.

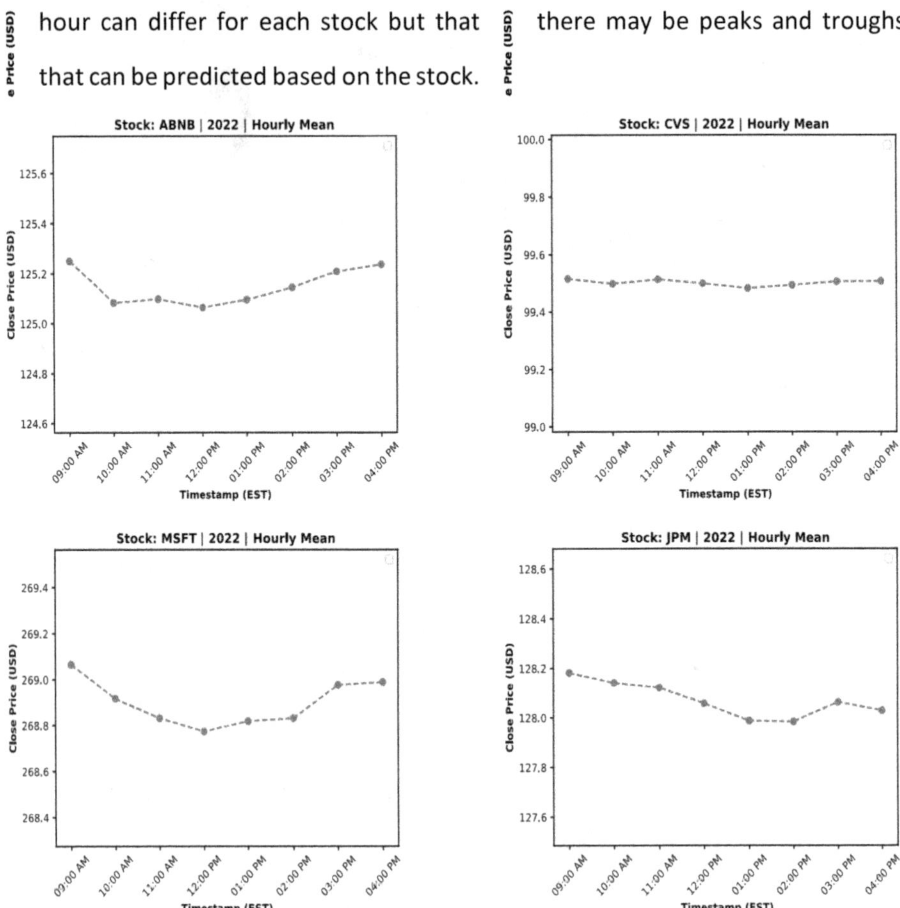

Figure 2: 2022 hourly stock price means for ABNB, CVS, MSFT and JPM

The mean and median prices were also plotted along with spread and outliers. The boxplots in figure 3 show the data distribution which comprise the mean values. The plot for JPM had outliers at every hour of the trading day. The mean price and spread are similar over all hours however there are slight differences. The data per hour over an entire year averages to about the same price so it is difficult to see the patterns in this zoomed out view. These plots show potential daily patterns that occur per stock. However, the zoomed in view of the mean price per hour in figure 2 reveal more pattern information than the boxplots. These plots are useful for seeing the average spread of the stock price per hour over 2022.

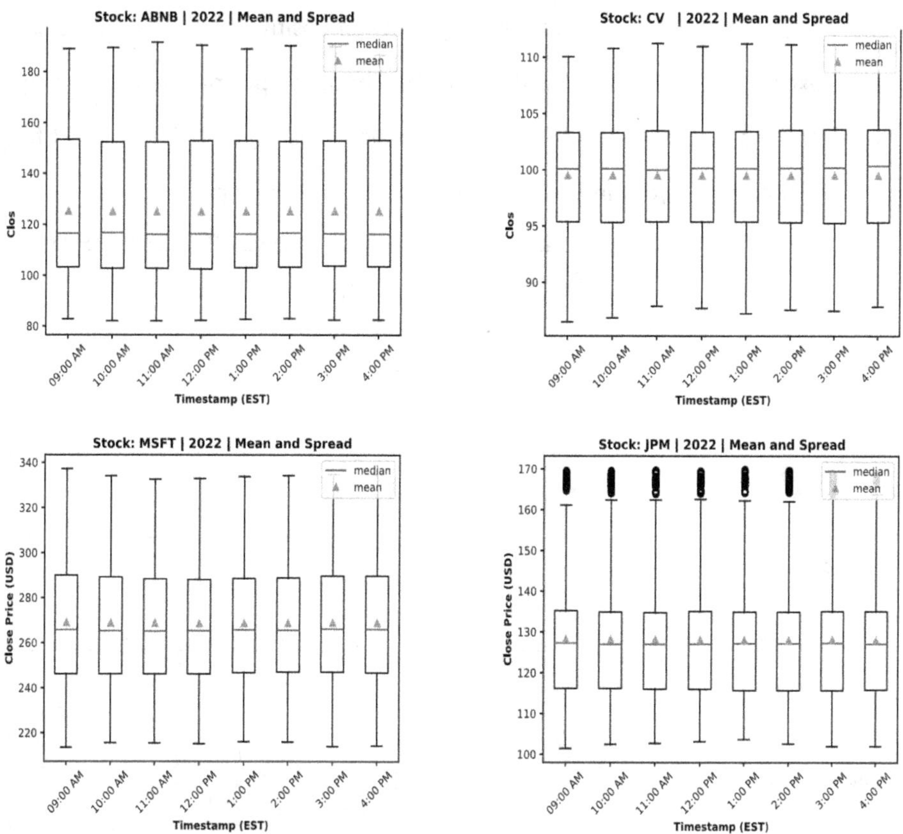

Figure 3: 2022 hourly stock price mean and spread for ABNB, CVS, MSFT and JPM

3.3 Hourly Mean Percent Change

The data was aggregated by hour over the entire year and the average change in price between the beginning and end of the hour was plotted as a percentage. While the percent change values are small, there are trends that can be seen on average

______________________________ for   a ___________

trading day. ABNB price went down over the first hour of the day but had a peak towards 11am. MSFT also started off with the price going down over the first few hours of the day but had a positive percent change between 2 and 3pm. CVS had each hour alternating between positive and negative percent change, except that 1pm to 2pm and 2pm to 3pm both had positive percent change. JPM started the day with a positive percent change, was negative for the next few hours and then had a peak in percent change between 3 and 4pm.

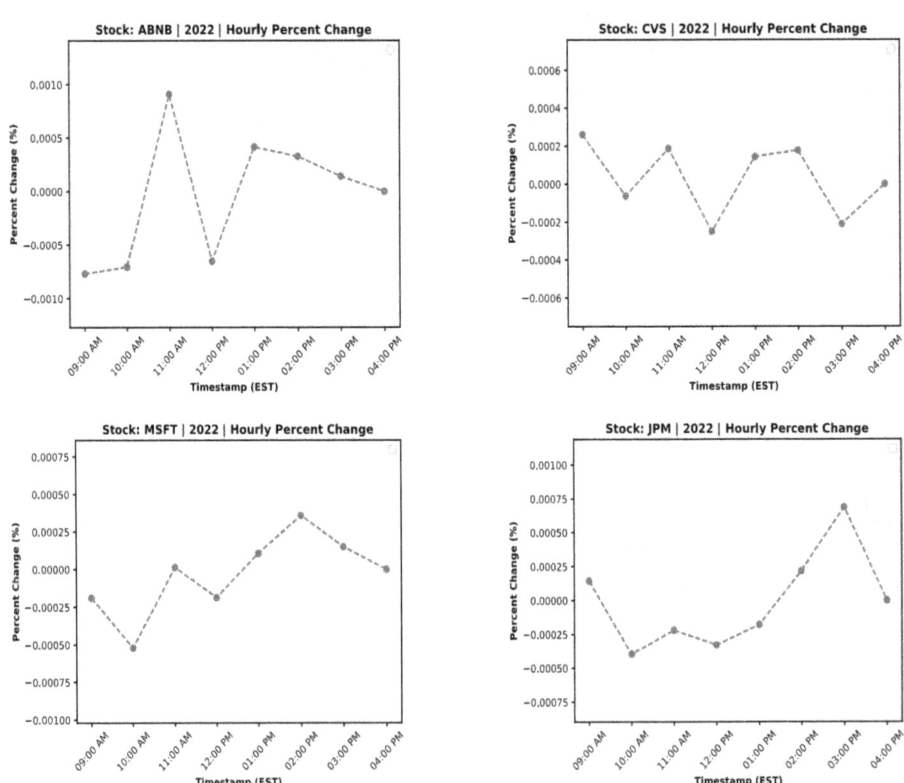

Figure 4: 2022 hourly percent change in price for ABNB, CVS, MSFT and JPM

3.4 Stock Splits

While doing preliminary data exploration some stocks appeared to have drastic drops in price. This was due to stock splitting. Two examples of stocks that split in 2022 can be seen in figure 5. It can be seen that Google's stock split in mid July and Tesla's stock split at end of August in 2022. Upon further investigation it was found that Google's stock split with a ratio of 20 to 1 on July 22, 2022 [26]. Tesla's stock split with a ratio of 3 to 1 on August 25, 2022 [26]. These splits and others will be addressed in the methods section.

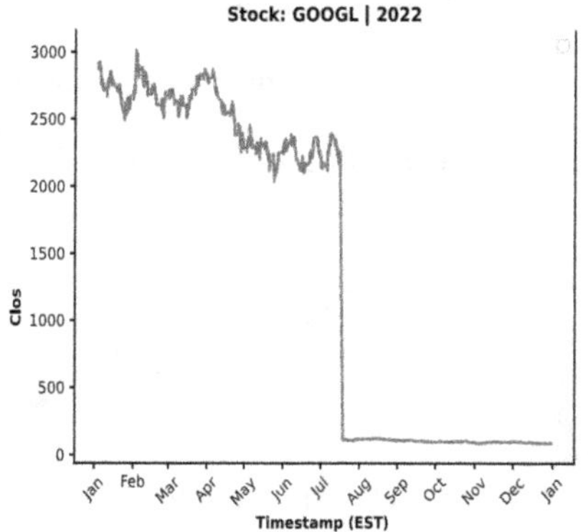

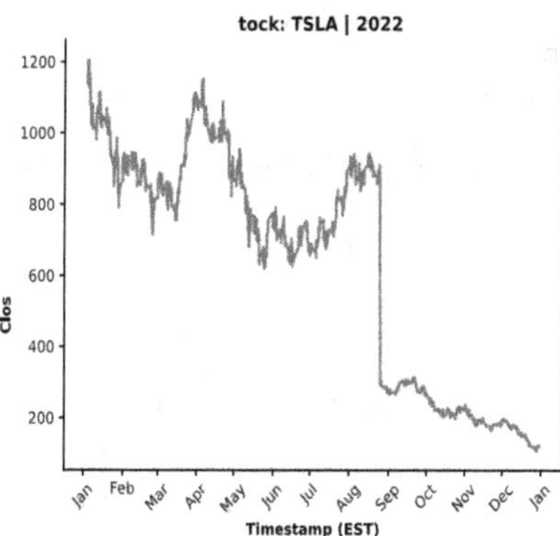

Figure 5: 2022 stock prices for GOOGL and TSLA

4   Methods

The goal of this section is to describe the methods that were used for testing the success of trading strategies over specified time period. Several trading algorithms were tested on stock market data and their results were recorded. These results, including number of trades and return on investment, became the input to ML models for prediction of success on subsequent time periods. The ML models were used to predict the success of each strategy, the best strategy for a given stock overall, the success of each strategy per hour of the trading day and the best trading strategy for a given stock per hour of the trading day. A trading simulation was done to test each strategy in practice on 18 stocks in a subsequent time period.

4.1 Machine Learning

Figure 6 shows the flow of data from collection to ML models. The red and blue lines show that the two datasets go through the same steps but separately. The four ML models were each run twice, once for the per stock data and once for the per stock per hour data.

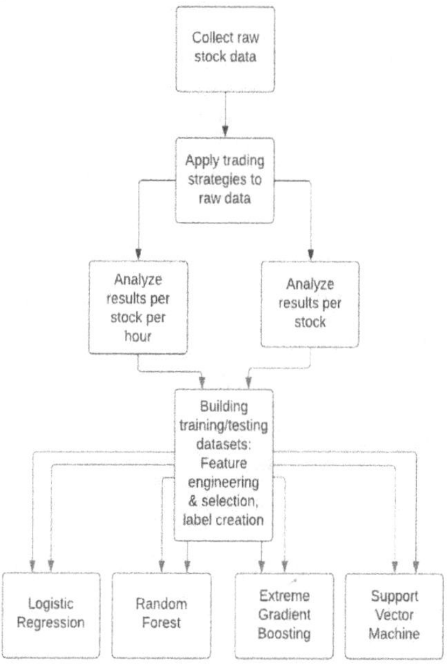

Figure 6: Data flow

4.1.1 Data Collection

Stocks Data was collected using stocks that are traded in the New York Stock Exchange (NYSE) and National Association of Securities Dealers Automated Quotations (NYSE) since they are the two largest stock exchanges in the world [27]. The top 802 stocks consisting of the highest 401 market cap stocks from NASDAQ and the highest 401 market cap stocks from NYSE were selected to be used for testing going forward. These stocks were selected since they tend to be the most established companies [28]. This list includes large well-known companies such as Google, Tesla and Amazon. The lists of NASDAQ stocks and NYSE stocks were downloaded from Stock Analysis. Each stock on the lists contained many values including financial indicators and company information. Some of these values were used and will be discussed in the training data section.

Historical price data Historical stock price data was collected for each of the 802 stocks selected. Stock market historical price data was collected using Alpaca Market Data API [29]. The data was collected for each stock in 6 month intervals at a 1 minute frequency. The data in each period of 6 months consisted of stock prices aggregated by minute throughout each day during trading hours. Each data point consisted of a timestamp, open price, close price, high price, low price, volume traded and volume weighted average price (vwap) aggregated over a minute. With 6.5 hours in a trading day (9:30am-4pm EST) and 60 minutes per hour, there were 60 * 6.5 = 390 data points per day per stock. The data in 6 month intervals was collected in the following 4 time periods over 2021-2023:

- t0: 7/1/2021 to 12/31/2021 • t1: 1/1/2022 to 6/30/2022

- t2: 7/1/2022 to 12/31/2022

- t3: 1/1/2023 to 6/30/2023

Some stocks did not have data available or did not have enough data for the given time periods. Some stocks had data for some time periods and not others. After collecting the data and removing stocks that did not have data in t0, t1 and t2, there were 770 stocks left that were used in the training and testing data sets. The data from t3 was saved for later use.

Quarterly Reports Quarterly and annual reports were collected for each of the 802 stocks using Alpha Vantage API [30]. The values that were used as features from the quarterly reports include total revenue, earnings before interest and taxes (EBIT) and earnings before interest, taxes, depreciation and amortization (EBITDA). These values were selected since they indicate a company's income and represent the company's profitability during a given time period [31] [32].

Stock Variety Although the top 802 companies were selected for the dataset, the companies were diverse in size and spanned multiple industries, sectors and states. The number of stocks broken down by these 5 categories can be seen in figure 7. These plots can be seen enlarged in Appendix E.

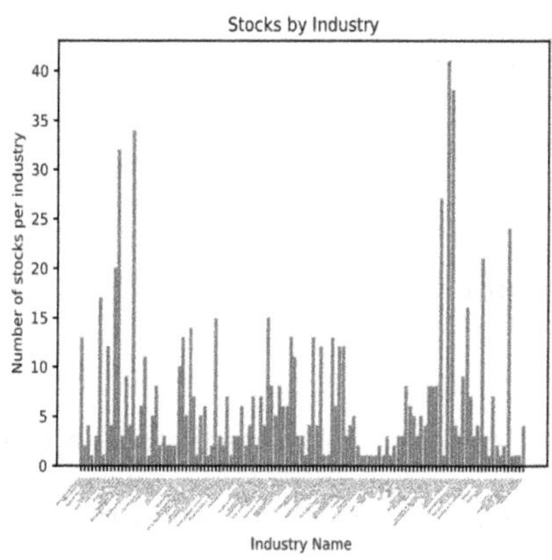

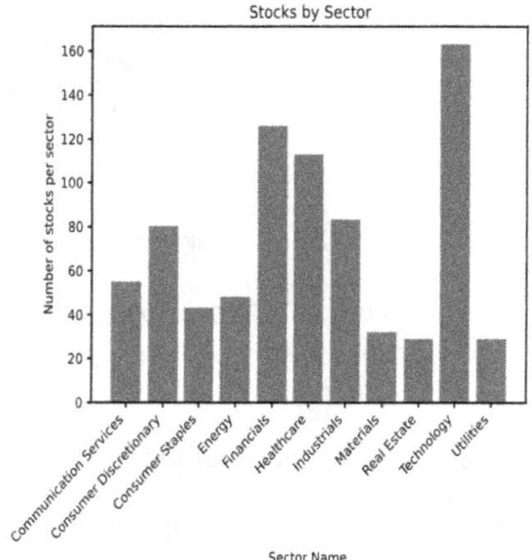

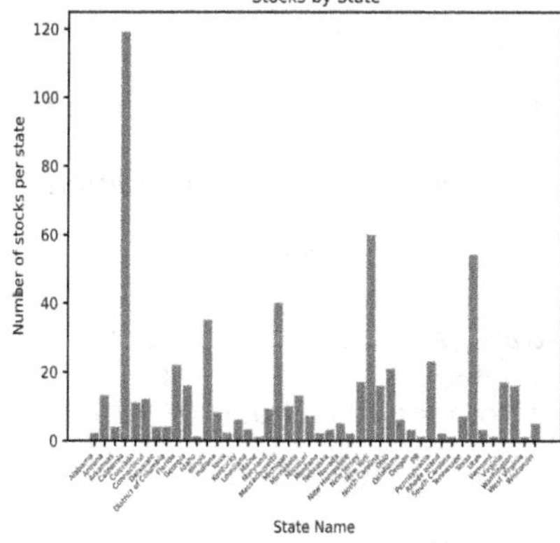

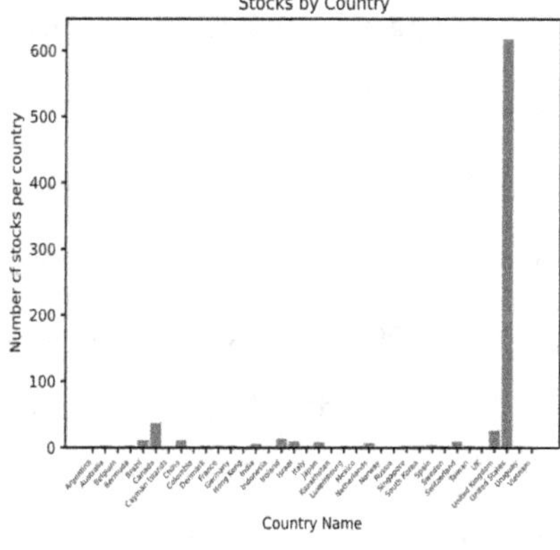

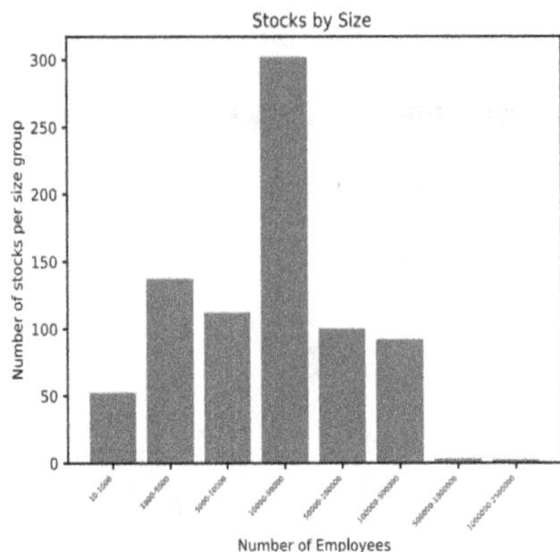

Figure 7: Breakdown of stocks by industry, sector, state, country and size

4.1.2 Building Training and Testing Datasets

Implementations of trading strategies Nine trading strategies were tested on the stock market data. The results of the trading strategies were included in the data for the machine learning models. The baseline trading strategy to which all methods were compared was buying a stock at the beginning of the trading day and selling it right before the trading day ended. This baseline is based on the basic definition of day trading in which stocks are bought and sold within a given day. In addition to this baseline, four other strategies were selected for testing. These four methods were each adapted into an additional trading strategy based on look-back periods which included data from previous days but only from the same hour of the day.

Stock Split As mentioned in the data exploration section some stocks split during the time periods analyzed. In these cases one stock became multiple stocks and the price of each stock became the original price divided by the split ratio. For example when Google's stock split in 2022 with a ratio of 20:1 each stock, worth $2,255.34 at the time, became 20 stocks with a price of about $2,255.34/20 = $112.76. In order to deal with this situation, the stock price from the split date forward was multiplied by the stock ratio so that instead of trading 1 share at a time, the number of shares traded at a time would be that multiple for the remaining duration of the 6 month period. More simply if 1 share of a stock was being traded and then it split, the new number of shares traded would be the split ratio.

Simple day trading strategy The simple day trading strategy was implemented as the baseline method. For simplicity, the times chosen were right after market open to buy and right before market closing to sell. Since the data was filtered to only contain stock prices during trading hours each day the buy and sell signals were generated for the baseline by taking the first and last data point of each day, respectively. This can be seen in the code snippet below.

```python
baseline_buy_signal = data.groupby(data.index.date).apply(lambda x: x.iloc[[0]
                                        ]) # first datapoint from each day
baseline_sell_signal = data.groupby(data.index.date).apply(lambda x: x.iloc[[-
                                        1]]) # last datapoint from each day
```

Simple Moving Average The simple moving average (SMA) crossover method and the SMA hourly version were implemented as the next two trading strategies. The long and short term

SMAs were computed for the SMA crossover trading strategy.

```python
sma_short = sma(data, 'close', f'{short_time_period}D') sma_long = sma(data,
'close', f'{long_time_period}D')
```

where the sma function is defined as:

```python
def sma(data, col, window):
    return data[col].rolling(window=window).mean()
```

The hourly version of this strategy worked the same way however the moving averages only included data from the same hour of the day as each data point. As seen in the code snippet below the data was grouped by hour and then the moving averages were computed.

```python
hourly_sma_short = ( data.groupby(data.index.hour)['close']
    .rolling(window=f'{short_time_period}D', min_periods=1)
    .mean()
    .reset_index(level=0, drop=True)
    )


hourly_sma_long = ( data.groupby(data.index.hour)['close']
    .rolling(window=f'{long_time_period}D', min_periods=1)
    .mean()
    .reset_index(level=0, drop=True)
    )
```

The crossover part of the trading strategy was the same for both adaptations after the moving averages were computed.

```python
crossover_signal = get_buy_and_sell_signals(sma_signal, f'sma_{short_time_period}_day', f'sma_{long_time_period}_day')
```

The get buy and sell signals function compares the input signals and returns the buy and sell signals.

```python
data['signal'] = np.where(data[col1] > data[col2], 1, 0)
```

Slow Stochastic Oscillator The slow stochastic oscillator method and the hourly adaptation were the next two trading strategies implemented. The code snippet below shows the implementation of the %K line equation and the %D line which is the moving average of the %K line.

```python
# Calculate the %K line stoch_osc['lowest_low'] = stoch_osc['low'].rolling(k).min()

stoch_osc['highest_high'] = stoch_osc['high'].rolling(k).max() stoch_osc['%K'] =

((stoch_osc['close'] - stoch_osc['lowest_low']) / (

                                        stoch_osc['highest_high']

                                        stoch_osc['lowest_low'])) * 100

# Calculate the %D line stoch_osc['%D'] =
stoch_osc['%K'].rolling(d).mean()
```

The hourly slow stochastic oscillator strategy was adapted from the slow stochastic oscillator method. Rather than computing the %K and %D lines based on entire day's min and max values the lines are computed at each hour of the day based on data only from the same hour during the previous days. The code snippets below show the implementation of this method.

```python
hourly_low = ( data.groupby(data.index.hour)['low']

    .rolling(window=k, min_periods=1)

    .min()

    .reset_index(level=0, drop=True)

    )




hourly_high = ( data.groupby(data.index.hour)['high']

    .rolling(window=k, min_periods=1)

    .max()

    .reset_index(level=0, drop=True)

    )
```

...

```python
hourly_osc['%K'] = ((hourly_osc['close'] - hourly_osc['lowest_low']) / (
                                            hourly_osc['highest_high']
                                            hourly_osc['lowest_low'] + 1e-10))
                                            * 100
# Calculate the %D line hourly_osc['%D'] =
hourly_osc['%K'].rolling(d).mean()
```

The trading rule implemented for both stochastic oscillator strategies can be seen in the code snippet below.

```python
stoch_osc.loc[(stoch_osc['%K'] < low_thresh) | (stoch_osc['%K'] >
                                stoch_osc['%D']), 'signal'] = 1
stoch_osc.loc[(stoch_osc['%K'] > high_thresh) | (stoch_osc['%K'] <
                                stoch_osc['%D']), 'signal'] = 0
```

A buy signal was generated when the %K line was above the %D line, similar to the SMA crossover method, or when the the %K line was below the low threshold. A sell signal was generated when the %K line was below the %D line or when the %K line was above the high threshold.

Mean Reversion The mean reversion and hourly mean reversion strategies were the next two trading strategies implemented. The z-score is computed on both a rolling basis over a given number of days and a rolling basis per hour over the same number of days.

```python
new_data['close_mean'] = new_data['close'].rolling(n_days).mean() new_data['deviation'] =
new_data['close'] - new_data['close_mean']

new_data['std_dev'] = (new_data['deviation'].pow(2)/new_data['close'].
                                rolling(n_days).count()).pow(1/2)
new_data['std_dev'] = new_data['std_dev'].replace(0, 1e-10) new_data['z_score'] =
new_data['deviation']/new_data['std_dev']
```

The hourly mean revision strategy was adapted to compute the z-score using hour specific means and standard deviations over the look back time period rather than using all of the data from the previous days to compute the mean and standard deviation at each timestamp.

```python
hourly_mean = ( data.groupby(data.index.hour)['close']
    .rolling(window=n_days, min_periods=1)
    .mean()
    .reset_index(level=0, drop=True)
    )


hourly_std_dev = ( data.groupby(data.index.hour)['close']
    .rolling(window=n_days, min_periods=1)
    .std()
    .reset_index(level=0, drop=True)
    )
```

The trading rule for mean reversion was to buy when the z-score was below a negative threshold and to sell when the z-score was above a positive threshold.

```python
hourly_data.loc[hourly_data['z_score'] < threshold[0], 'signal'] = 1
hourly_data.loc[hourly_data['z_score'] > threshold[1], 'signal'] = 0
```

Relative Strength Index   The RSI and hourly RSI indicators were computed in a similar way to the other strategies.

```python
price_differences = data[col].diff() gain =
price_differences.where(price_differences > 0, 0)
```

```python
loss = -price_differences.where(price_differences < 0, 0)


avg_gain = gain.rolling(window=period).mean() avg_loss =

loss.rolling(window=period).mean()


rs = avg_gain / avg_loss rsi = 100 -
(100 / (1 + rs))
```

The hourly RSI strategy was adapted to use average price differences calculated per hour rather than per entire day.

```python
hourly_gain = ( data.groupby(data.index.hour)['gain']

    .rolling(window=n_days, min_periods=1)

    .mean()

    .reset_index(level=0, drop=True)

    )


hourly_loss = ( data.groupby(data.index.hour)['loss']

    .rolling(window=n_days, min_periods=1)

    .mean()

    .reset_index(level=0, drop=True)

    )
```

The trading rule was implemented based on thresholds. When the RSI value was below a low threshold a share was bought. When the RSI was above a high threshold a share was sold.

```python
new_data.loc[new_data['rsi'] < low_thresh, 'signal'] = 1 new_data.loc[new_data['rsi'] >

high_thresh, 'signal'] = 0
```

4.1.3 Trading Strategy Examples

Figure 8 shows an example of the simple day trading strategy applied to ABNB over
the year 2022.

Figure 8: Simple Day Trading Strategy for ABNB 2022

Examples of the remaining trading strategy signals along with original data can
be seen for ABNB as an example in figure 9. The z-score in the mean reversion signal
plot varies to high and low extremes so it is difficult to see the low and high
thresholds at -1.5 and 1.5 standard deviations, respectively. These lines can be seen
clearly in the mean reversion hourly signal plot.

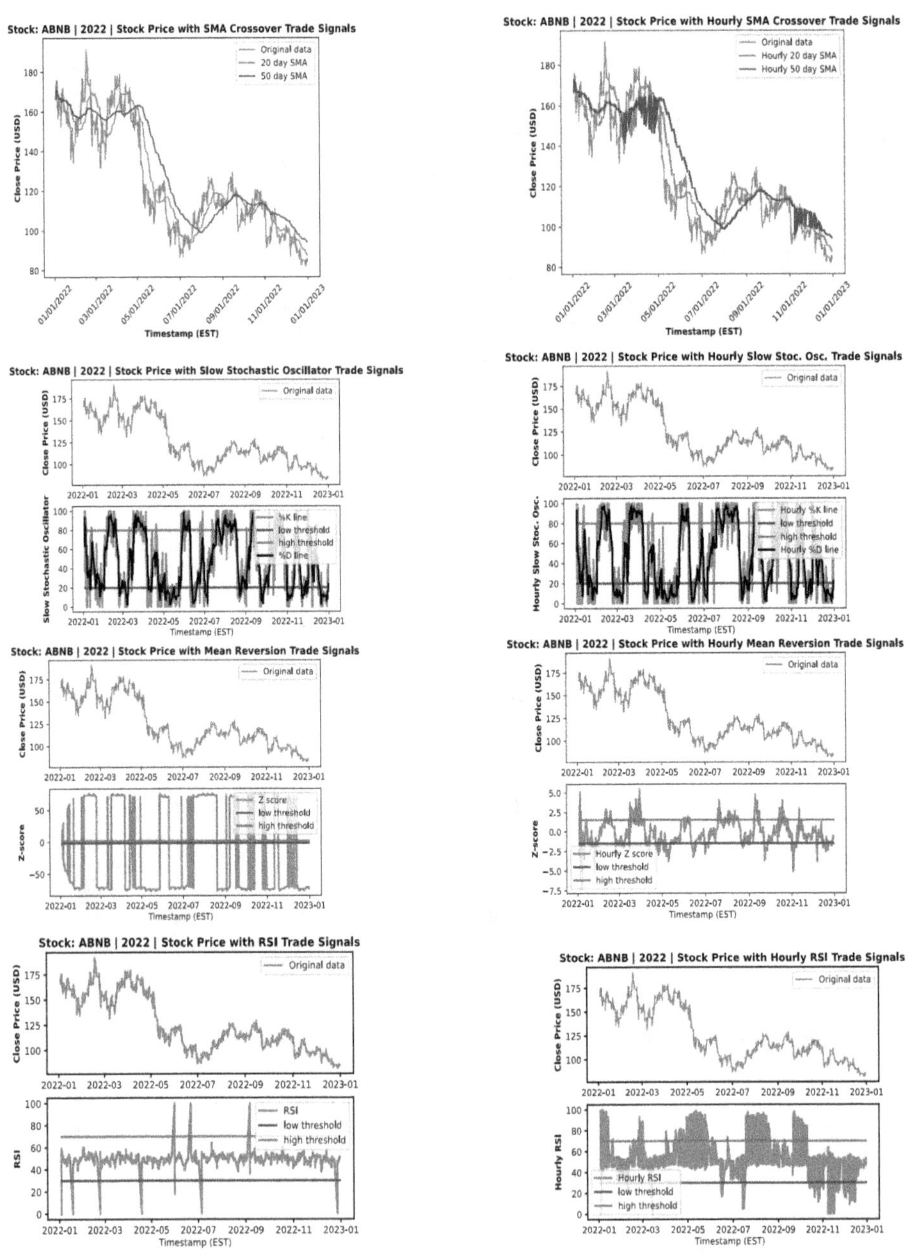

Figure 9: Trading Strategies for ABNB 2022

Figure 10 shows the total profits per hour and total trades per hour for each strategy over 2022 for ABNB. These plots show a visual overview of the performance of each trading strategy for ABNB.

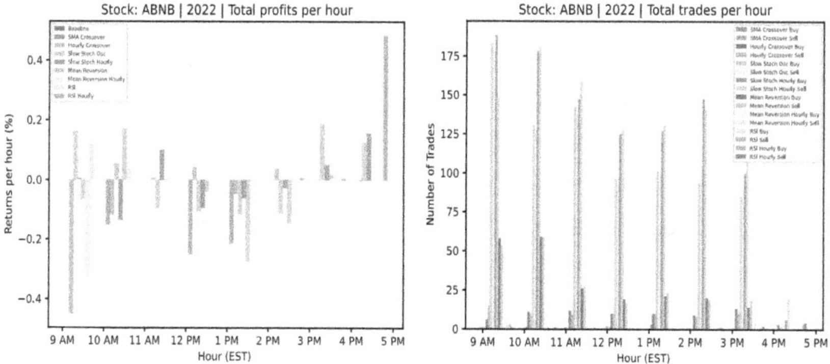

Figure 10: Hourly Profits and Trades for ABNB 2022

Data pre-processing - applying trading strategies The raw data was pre-processed by running each stock's data through each of the 9 trading strategies for each of the four time periods. The total profits in dollar value, return on investment (%), total number of buys and total number of sells were computed for each of the stocks in the training data. The total profits represent the money made in dollars (USD) due to buying and selling 1 share of a stock over the given 6 month period. The total returns are the profits as percentage of money invested due to buying and selling 1 share of a stock over the given 6 month period. The total buys and sells represent the number of times the share was bought and sold during the 6 month period, respectively. Only 1 of each share was traded at a time for each trading strategy, meaning there was never more than 1 share in ownership at a time, with the exception of a stock split occurring. A buy only occurred if the previous position was a sell.

The data was also analyzed on an hourly basis. The results of the trading strategies were aggregated over the hours of a trading day. The total profits per hour, returns per hour, buys per hour and sells per hour were computed and used as a dataset broken down by hour. The total profits and returns per hour for a stock represent the total amount of money and percentage of money made in each hour over the 6 month period. The total buys and sells per hour represent the total number of times a share was bought or sold during each hour of the trading day over the 6 month period.

Feature SelectionThe feature set includes 4 categories of data.

- The results of each trading strategy on the raw data

- Summary statistics of the stock in the given time period

- Time independent data about the company

- Values related to earnings from the quarterly reports

For the per stock data and the per hour data, the features from the tradings strategy results included for each trading strategy, the total profits, total returns, total buys and total sells. The per hour data had the added feature of hour of the day (9 through 16).

These feature names were formatted as:

- '{strategy name} profits'

- '{strategy name} returns'

- '{strategy name} totalbuys'

- '{strategy name} total_sells'

With 9 strategies and these 4 feature categories, these account for 36 of the features in each feature set.

The summary statistics used were mean price, standard deviation, high value and low value. For the dataset broken down by hour, these values were computed separately for each hour in the trading day over each 6 month period.

The time independent variables that were used include state, country, company size (can change but general values remain), industry, sector, stock exchange, whether or not the stock gives a dividend, year the company was founded, year the company went public and the IPO price.

An example of one row of the per stock training data can be seen below in table 1.

Feature name	value	Feature name	value	Feature name	value	baseline profits	26.7884	baseline total buys	163
Founded	1977.0	sma profits	0.0	sma total buys	1	gives dividend	1	sma hourly profits 9.9137 sma hourly total buys	
25 Employees	161000.0	stoch profits	3.0836	stoch total buys	390	country Argentina	0		
stoch hourly profits	-3.1797	stoch hourly total buys	394	… mean rever profits	14.5782				
mean rever total buys	220	country United States	1						
mean rever hourly profits	15.6481	mean rever hourly total buys	21	…					
rsi profits	0.0	rsi total buys	0	sector Technology	1				
rsi hourly profits	28.827	rsi hourly total buys	33	…					
baseline returns	0.196611	baseline total sells	163	industry Consumer Electronics	1				
sma returns	0.0	sma total sells	1	…					
sma hourlyreturns 0.066087 sma hourly total sells 25 state California 1 stoch returns 0.016611 stoch total sells 390									
…									
stoch hourlyreturns -0.029371 stoch hourly total sells 394 ebit 65855000000.0 mean reverreturns 0.094617 mean rever total sells 219 ebitda 70960000000.0 mean reverhourly returns 0.106132 mean rever hourly total sells 20 totalRevenue 205939000000.0 rsi returns 0.0 rsi total sells 0 mean price 147.366601 rsi hourly returns 0.205916 rsi hourly total sells 33 std dev 13.883965									
IPO Year	1980.0	exchange NASDAQ	1	low	122.25				
IPO Price	NaN	exchange NYSE	0	high	182.13				

Table 1: Feature values for one data point

Table 2 shows an example of one data point in the hourly dataset. Some of the features overlap with the per stock data while some are unique to the hourly data. For example, hour, '{strategy name} returns _buy' and '{strategy name} profits buy' features are unique to hourly data. The '{strategy name} returns buy' and '{strategy name} profits buy' features represent the returns and profits, respectively, that were made upon selling later due to buying at the specified hour. The '{strategy name} _profits' and '{strategy name} returns' features represent the returns and profits, respectively, that were made upon selling at the specified hour.

Feature name	value	Feature name	value	Feature name	value
baseline profits	0.0	baseline returns	0.0	baseline total sells	0
sma profits	0.0	sma _returns	0.0	sma total sells	0
sma hourly profits	2.8187	sma _hourly returns	0.019305	sma hourly _total sells	1
stoch profits	-1.1309	stoch returns	-0.007722	stoch total sells	62
stoch hourly _profits	-4.224	stoch hourly returns	-0.029545	stoch hourly total sells	59
mean _rever profits	6.7763	mean rever returns	0.045222	mean rever total sells	33
mean rever hourly profits	5.0745	mean rever hourly returns	0.033803	mean rever hourly total sells	5
rsi profits	0.0	rsi returns	0.0	rsi total sells	0
rsi hourly _profits	0.1915	rsi hourly returns	0.00123	rsi hourly total sells	1
baseline profits buy	0.0	baseline returns buy	0.0	baseline total buys	0
sma profits buy	0.0	sma returns-buy	0.0	sma total buys	0
sma hourly profits buy	2.8187	sma _hourly returns buy	0.019305	sma hourly _total buys	1
stoch profits buy	-7.0585	stoch returns buy	-0.044881	stoch total buys	57
stoch hourly _profits buy	-5.2843	stoch hourly returns _buy	-0.03593	stoch hourly total buys	61
mean _rever profits buy	1.9972	mean rever returns buy	0.01377	mean rever total buys	44
mean rever hourly profits buy	-7.7215	mean rever hourly returns buy	-0.049718	mean rever hourly total buys	5
rsi profits buy	0.0	rsi returns buy	0.0	rsi total buys	0
rsi hourly _profits buy	0.5727	rsi hourly returns buy	0.003686	rsi hourly total buys	2
hour	10	gives dividend	1	Founded	1977.0
ebit	65855000000.0	ebitda	70960000000.0	totalRevenue	205939000000.0
country Argentina	0	...		...	
...		sector Technology	1	state _California	1
country United States	1	...		...	
...		industry _Consumer Electronics	1	mean price	147.318119
exchange NASDAQ	1	...		std dev	13.850711
exchange NYSE	0	IPO Price	NaN	low	122.83
Employees	161000.0	IPO Year	1980.0	high	182.13

Table 2: Feature values for one data point - hourly

The examples in tables 1 and 2 show the original values of each feature before they are scaled and normalized. The 'returns' features are in decimal value rather than percent.

Feature Engineering Features were engineered to make sure they would work well with the models. Some of the features included categorical data that were not numeric in nature. These features were industry, sector, stock market exchange, state and country. All of these features were in the form of strings and needed to be encoded in a way that preserves the validity of the data. One hot encoding was used on these features. This created n new features to replace each feature where n is the number of unique values in each category (of each feature). Each new feature consisted of binary values to represent whether or not the given stock had that feature value. For example, instead of having "exchange" as a feature with values "NYSE" and "NASDAQ", 2 new features replaced it: "exchange NYSE" and "exchange NASDAQ" each with values 0 and 1 representing if the stock belongs to either of those stock exchanges.

The data needed to be normalized so that the different scales, units and values of each feature would be relative to one another and be compared properly. The total profits for each strategy and stock were based on trading 1 share of each stock throughout the 6 month time period. Therefore, the total profits were based on each stock's price. To normalize this feature the total profits of each stock were divided the mean price of the given stock. This changed the feature to a fraction of mean stock price which allowed comparison between each stock and made the feature in one scale. The returns features were already in percentages so they were left as is. The features needed to be scaled in relation to one another as well. Since there were already many features with binary values all of the other features were normalized to be between 0 and 1 by doing min max scaling.

Trading Strategy Parameter Optimization Each trading strategy had specific parameters such as moving average look-back periods and trading value thresholds. The look-back periods and smoothing windows were optimized for best results. A custom grid search of parameters was done for each strategy. Each stock's data was put through each of the 8 non baseline trading strategies with multiple combinations of parameters. The total returns from time period t0 were computed and the parameters that most frequently gave the highest total profits were recorded for each stock. The parameters for each strategy that produced the highest returns most frequently were selected as the parameters for the strategies going forward in all time periods. Table 3 shows the optimal parameters from time period t0 for all of the trading strategies. Strategies that contained a long and short look-back period have values filled in for both columns. Strategies that only have one look-back period only have a value filled in for the 'short time period' column.

Strategy	Short time period (days)	Long time period (days)
SMA	20	50
SMA Hourly	20	50
Stochastic Oscillator	3	14
Stochastic Oscillator Hourly	3	14
Mean Reversion	5	
Mean Reversion Hourly	5	
RSI	3	
RSI Hourly	3	

Table 3: Optimal trading strategy parameters

The optimal parameters ended up being the same for each strategy and its hourly version interestingly. Many of the optimal parameters were the same as the typical values initially used. However, when looking at the optimal parameters based on t1, the values were not the same as t0. The best parameters based on t0 were used going forward for consistency. The look-back period parameters were optimized.

The threshold values were not optimized due to the exponential increase in operations that would need to be done to test several values of thresholds with several values of time periods. The standard threshold values were used going forward.

Hyperparameter Tuning The Machine learning models have many parameters based on each specific classification algorithm. Some of these parameters were tuned using a grid search. For logistic regression the solver, penalty and C value were tuned. For random forest n estimators, max depth, min samples split and min samples leaf were tuned. For XGB n estimators, max depth and learning _rate were tuned. For SVM the kernel, degree and C values were tuned. This added significant time to training the models.

Label Creation The labels for the datasets were created during the feature generation step in the process. The returns that were computed for each stock during each time period were turned into binary values representing if each strategy was profitable for each stock. For the hourly data, the returns were computed at each hour per stock when selling shares and the returns were computed at each buy signal based on how well selling those shares ended up performing. The code snippet below shows how the 'is _profitable' labels were created for the per stock data.

```python
is_profitable.append(int(returns_signal > 0))
```

The code snippets below show how the labels were created for the hourly data for both selling and buying.

```python
hourly_df[f'{strategy}_is_prof'] = (hourly_returns > 0).astype(int)
```

...

```
hourly_df[f'{strategy}_is_prof_buy'] = (hourly_returns_buys > 0).astype(
int)
```

The best strategy overall and the best strategy per hour for both buying and selling were also used as labels. These were created by choosing the strategies that resulted in highest returns overall during each time period.

Time periods used- linking features and labels The features in the t0 data were paired with the labels in t1. This is because the goal was to use the data from a period of 6 months to predict the behavior of trading strategies on those stocks in the subsequent 6 months. Therefore the training dataset included t0 features with t1 labels and the testing data included t1 features with t2 labels.

Figure 11 shows the structure of features and labels using each time period.

Figure 11: Structure of features and labels

Transaction Fee When computing the returns a transaction fee was not included. This is because many large brokerage firms including Charles Schwabb, Robinhood, TD Ameritrade and JP Morgan no longer charge a commission fee for online trading [33]. Therefore it would be simple to replicate these results without having to pay any transaction fees or commissions.

4.1.4 ML Models

Logistic regression, random forest, extreme gradient boosting and support vector machine were each tested for their ability to classify each strategy as profitable or not profitable and to determine the best strategy in a 9 label classification problem where each label was a different trading strategy. These models were optimized and used for both the overall predictions and the hourly predictions for each stock in the dataset.

4.1.5 Hourly method vs per stock

Stock trading strategies were tested on stocks using ML and a trading simulation to mimic realtime trading. Both methods were analyzed by looking at how the trading strategies performed for each stock overall and how well they performed for each stock at each hour of the trading day.

4.1.6 Model Metrics and Analysis

The machine learning models were scored using four different metrics. The metrics include accuracy score, precision score, recall score and f1 score.

Accuracy score is a measure of total correct predictions based on comparing the actual class labels and predicted class labels. It measures how many labels were predicted correctly. Equation 12 shows the computation used for accuracy score.

$$accuracy(y, \hat{y}) = \frac{1}{n_{samples}} \sum_{i=0}^{n_{samples}-1} 1(\hat{y}_i = y_i) \tag{12}$$

where $1(x)$ is equal to 1 if $\hat{y}_i = y_i$ and is equal to 0 if $\hat{y}_i = y_i$. The range of values is 0 to 1 where 1 means all labels were predicted correctly.

Precision score measures the ability of a classifier to not produce false positives. Equation 13 shows the computation used for precision score. A low precision score indicates a high rate of

false positives.

$$precision = \frac{true\_positives}{true\_positives + false\_positives} \tag{13}$$

Recall score measures the ability of a classifier to not produce false negatives. Equation 14 shows the computation used for recall score. A low recall score indicates a high rate of false

negatives.

$$recall = \frac{true\_positives}{true\_positives + false\_negatives} \tag{14}$$

F1 score represents a balanced calculation or harmonic average between precision and recall. Equation 15 shows the calculation used for this metric.

$$F1 = 2 * \frac{precision * recall}{precision + recall} \tag{15}$$

4.2 Simulation

Until now the stocks were tested by simulating a trade of 1 share at a time. To make it more realistic this simulation allowed $1000 for each stock and strategy. In order to test out our hypothesis and results 18 stocks were selected from our original top 802 stocks that were used in the ML training and testing data. Each stock and strategy was tested to see how they would perform with $1000.

4.2.1 Stock selection

18 stocks were selected from the original 802 top market cap stocks for further analysis and testing. Both NASDAQ and NYSE stocks were selected from multiple industries and sectors. These stocks included: TSLA, TM, SBUX, AMZN, MSFT, ORCL, AMAT, TSM, MRNA, JNJ, WMT, COST, UNH, CVS, JPM, PYPL, PEP, and KO. Table 4 shows each stock symbol along with its company name, industry and stock exchange.

Stock Symbol	Company Name	Industry	Exchange
AMAT	Applied Materials, Inc.	Semiconductor Equipment & Materials	NASDAQ
AMZN	Amazon.com, Inc.	Internet Retail	NASDAQ
COST	Costco Wholesale Corporation	Discount Stores	NASDAQ
CVS	CVS Health Corporation	Healthcare Plans	NYSE
JPM	JPMorgan Chase & Co.	Banks - Diversified	NYSE
JNJ	Johnson & Johnson	Drug Manufacturers - General	NYSE
KO	The Coca-Cola Company	Beverages - Non-Alcoholic	NYSE
MRNA	Moderna, Inc.	Biotechnology	NASDAQ
MSFT	Microsoft Corporation	Software - Infrastructure	NASDAQ
ORCL	Oracle Corporation	Software - Infrastructure	NYSE
PEP	PepsiCo, Inc.	Beverages - Non-Alcoholic	NASDAQ
PYPL	PayPal Holdings, Inc.	Credit Services	NASDAQ
SBUX	Starbucks Corporation	Restaurants	NASDAQ
TM	Toyota Motor Corporation	Auto Manufacturers	NYSE
TSLA	Tesla, Inc.	Auto Manufacturers	NASDAQ
TSM	Taiwan Semiconductor Manufacturing Company Limited	Semiconductors	NYSE
UNH	UnitedHealth Group Incorporated	Healthcare Plans	NYSE
WMT	Walmart Inc.	Discount Stores	NYSE

Table 4: Stock Symbols

Data from time period t3 (1/1/2023 to 6/30/2023) was used for this set of testing. The data from this time period was not used in the ML training or testing data so it was specifically reserved for this simulation.

4.3 Pre-simulation ML

The ML models that performed the best were used to predict the results of the simulation. For the per stock data an SVM model was used and for the hourly data the logistic regression model was used. The ML models were trained using t1 features with t2 labels for the training data and t2 features with t3 labels as the testing data. The testing and training data were built the same way as in the previous section, however the subsequent time periods were used. The testing data became the training data and the new testing data included the features from time period t2 with the labels from time period t3.

4.3.1 Simulation steps

The simulation was done to mimic live trading. For each stock all nine strategy signals were computed. In an actual live test the strategy signals would be computed at each minute, however for simplicity the signals were computed on the entire 6 months. The original data was looped through each minute for every stock. At each minute, the strategy signal was checked to see if the stock was in a buy or sell position. If this position was different from the previous position then a trade was 'executed' and recorded. If a trade was made then the total account value, total cash and the strategy used were recorded. Up to $1000 worth of shares were traded at a time regardless of the stock and its price. The quantity of shares bought and sold can be seen in the code snippet below.

```
quantity = investment_amount / current_ask_price
```

If any extra profit was made on a sell, it was stored and not used for subsequent trades, ensuring a

$1000 limit. If money was lost then the new total less than $1000 was used for subsequent trades.

Each simulated trade was recorded and analyzed afterwards.

4.3.2 Simulation metrics and analysis

The results from the tradeing simulation were compared to the predictions made by the ML models. Accuracy scores were computed for each label. The label predictions were cross referenced with the results from the simulation to determine if the ML model correctly predicted the outcome of the simulation.

5 Results

The resulting values for the metrics described in the previous section are presented in this section. For the 'is profitable' labels the baseline accuracy score is 50% because random guessing probabilistically translates to 50% accuracy. The baseline accuracy for the 'best strategy' labels is 11.11% because random guessing out of 9 strategies translates to 1/9 or 11.11% accuracy. The percentages in the following results indicate the degree of accuracy to which the ML models can predict whether or not a trading strategy will be successful for that stock and time period. Some of the accuracy scores indicate the degree to which one of the nine strategies can be predicted as best for a stock over a period of time.

5.1 ML Results

The results of the ML models were quantified based on accuracy, precision and recall and F1 scores as described in the methods section. The values can be seen for each label and model. The metrics for the is profitable labels were averaged together over all the models and the metrics for the best strategy labels were averaged together over all the models to get an overview of the results.

The results for the logistic regression model can be seen in table 5. The baseline is prof, mean rever is prof, mean rever _hourly is _prof and rsi hourly is prof labels all had accuracy scores below 50%. This means that predicting the success of these three labels performed worse than randomly guessing if each of those strategies would be profitable or not profitable. The sma is prof, sma hourly is prof, stoch is prof, stoch hourly is prof and rsi is prof labels all had accuracy values above 50% which means that their success was able to be predicted to some degree. The rsi _is prof strategy had the highest accuracy score of 87.27%, however precision and recall have values of 0 indicating that there were no true positives predicted and that the accuracy comes from correctly predicting that the strategy was not profitable. The sma is prof label had a high value for both accuracy and precision indicating that true positives were able to be predicted. The best strategy label had an accuracy score of 19.09% which means that predicting best strategy overall was better than randomly selecting a strategy.

Label	Accuracy	Precision	Recall	F1
baseline is prof	38.18	53.22	18.69	27.66
sma is prof	60.91	53.85	2.32	4.44
sma hourly is prof	57.40	0.00	0.00	0.00
stoch is prof	54.81	52.94	20.22	29.27
stoch hourly is prof	55.19	66.67	1.72	3.36
mean rever is prof	46.62	84.11	24.71	38.20
mean rever hourly is prof	44.68	78.95	12.77	21.98
rsi is prof	87.27	0.00	0.00	0.00
rsi hourly is _prof	37.53	59.46	4.51	8.38

Label	Accuracy	Precision	Recall	F1
best strategy	19.09	14.47	13.82	11.15

Table 5: Logistic Regression Results

The results for random forest can be seen in table 6. The results are similar to the logistic regression results in that the same strategies performed below and above 50% accuracy. The best strategy label had an accuracy score of 20.0% which is better than random guessing and better than the same result using logistic regression.

Label	Accuracy	Precision	Recall	F1
baseline is prof	41.04	66.02	13.96	23.05
sma is prof	60.78	50.00	2.65	5.03
sma hourly is prof	57.14	40.00	1.22	2.37
stoch is prof	55.58	55.56	19.66	29.05
stoch hourly is prof	56.49	55.65	18.39	27.65
mean rever is prof	47.27	70.45	36.19	47.81
mean rever hourly is prof	47.53	65.57	29.57	40.76
rsi is prof	87.01	0.00	0.00	0.00
rsi hourly is prof	37.66	68.18	3.07	5.88
best strategy	20.00	9.91	12.09	7.68

Table 6: Random Forest Results

The results for XGB can be seen in 7. The labels performed similarly to the previous two models in terms of each label being above or below 50% accuracy. The best strategy label performed worse than the previous two models with an accuracy score of 17.79% but was still better than random guessing.

Label	Accuracy	Precision	Recall	F1
baseline is prof	41.30	61.74	18.89	28.93
sma is prof	60.91	66.67	0.66	1.31
sma hourly is prof	57.40	0.00	0.00	0.00
stoch is prof	55.97	54.03	32.02	40.21
stoch hourly is prof	54.81	0.00	0.00	0.00
mean rever is prof	38.05	74.03	11.09	19.29
mean rever hourly is prof	42.60	70.00	10.43	18.15
rsi is prof	87.27	0.00	0.00	0.00
rsi hourly is prof	38.83	67.35	6.76	12.29
best strategy	17.79	9.92	12.75	8.93

Table 7: XGBoost Results

The SVM results can be seen in 8. Almost all of the labels in these results are also similar to the previous results. However, in these results the mean rever is prof label was predicted with an accuracy of 54.16% while in the previous results this label performed below 50% accuracy. Furthermore this label had a 77.29% recall which is a relatively high value in these results. The best strategy label performed better than the previous results with an accuracy score of 22.34% and was better than random guessing.

Label	Accuracy	Precision	Recall	F1
baseline is prof	41.04	61.70	17.86	27.71
sma is prof	60.91	53.85	2.32	4.44
sma hourly is prof	57.40	0.00	0.00	0.00
stoch is prof	56.10	64.06	11.52	19.52
stoch hourly is prof	56.10	60.42	8.33	14.65
mean rever is prof	54.16	77.29	44.36	56.37
mean rever hourly is prof	46.62	78.64	17.23	28.27
rsi is prof	86.49	12.50	1.02	1.89
rsi hourly is _prof	40.78	68.18	12.30	20.83
best strategy	22.34	2.49	11.11	4.06

Table 8: SVM Results

The results for hourly predictions using logistic regression can be seen in 9. All of the labels except rsi hourly is prof buy performed better than the random guessing baseline. The baseline is prof buy and mean rever is prof buy labels performed well with high accuracy values and reasonably high precision. The best strategy buy and best strategy _sell labels performed better than random guessing and better than the similar labels in the non hourly data.

Label	Accuracy	Precision	Recall	F1

baseline is prof	83.54	0.00	0.00	0.00
sma is prof	91.61	0.00	0.00	0.00
sma hourly is prof	53.93	25.00	0.46	0.91
stoch is prof	62.34	58.62	2.91	5.54
stoch hourly is prof	61.92	73.07	30.91	43.44
mean rever is prof	64.74	67.52	81.80	73.98
mean rever hourly _is prof	59.29	54.81	79.52	64.89
rsi is prof	98.34	0.00	0.00	0.00
rsi hourly is prof	59.14	60.80	75.46	67.34
baseline is prof buy	92.18	54.34	18.91	28.06
sma is prof buy	91.53	0.00	0.00	0.00
sma hourly is prof buy	57.55	0.00	0.00	0.00
stoch is prof buy	57.78	42.32	4.85	8.70
stoch hourly is prof buy	57.81	57.89	0.84	1.66
mean rever is prof buy	65.49	67.19	88.55	76.40
mean rever hourly is prof	56.62	57.92	47.20	52.01
buy rsi is prof buy	98.36	0.00	0.00	0.00
rsi hourly is prof buy	46.56	54.72	43.60	48.53
best strategy sell	30.49	14.83	16.31	11.90
best strategy buy	28.59	18.81	14.30	10.43

Table 9: Logistic Regression Hourly Results

The results for random forest hourly predictions can be seen in table 10. Again, of the labels except rsi hourly is prof buy performed better than the random guessing baseline of 50%. The rsi _is prof (sell) and rsi is prof buy labels had high accuracies but 0 precision. This indicates potential class imbalance in the data or inability to predict any positive values. The sma is prof buy and baseline is prof _buy performed well. Random forest performed well with best strategy buy and best strategy sell beating the baseline (11%) and the similar labels in the non hourly data.

| | Accuracy | Precision | Recall | F1 |
Label				
baseline is prof	83.64	51.85	8.28	14.29
sma is prof sma hourly is prof	91.53	0.00	0.00	0.00
stoch is prof	54.25	42.86	0.64	1.26
stoch hourly is prof	59.79	43.56	19.79	27.21
	56.92	68.10	16.84	27.01
mean rever is prof	58.08	62.64	78.27	69.59
mean rever hourly _is prof	53.91	53.42	20.34	29.47
rsi is prof	98.34	0.00	0.00	0.00
rsi hourly is prof	51.85	56.31	61.38	58.74
baseline is prof buy	91.87	45.45	4.02	7.39
sma is prof buy	87.68	8.71	4.79	6.18
sma hourly is prof buy	48.10	37.85	34.68	36.20
stoch is prof buy	58.25	40.00	1.25	2.43
stoch hourly is prof buy	55.37	43.71	19.19	26.67
mean rever is prof buy	65.24	67.17	87.86	76.13
mean rever hourly is prof	50.60	54.18	5.28	9.62
buy rsi is prof buy	98.36	0.00	0.00	0.00
rsi hourly is prof buy	42.56	58.87	2.05	3.96
best strategy sell	29.04	23.58	15.50	11.72
best strategy buy	24.12	12.00	13.42	10.42

Table 10: Random Forest Hourly Results

The results for XGB hourly predictions can be seen in table 11. Again, all of the labels except rsi hourly is prof buy performed better than the random guessing baseline of 50%. The sma is _prof (sell), sma hourly _is prof (sell), rsi is prof (sell) and rsi is prof buy labels had high accuracy values but 0 precision. Again, the stoch is prof and stoch hourly is prof labels performed well with above 50% accuracy and above 50% precision. The baseline is prof buy performed well again with 92.09% accuracy and 55% precision. The best strategy sell beat baseline and the non hourly results

Label	Accuracy	Precision	Recall	F1
baseline is prof	79.64	38.68	40.43	39.54
sma is prof sma hourly is prof	91.61	0.00	0.00	0.00
stoch is prof	54.35	0.00	0.00	0.00
stoch hourly is prof	62.06	53.49	0.98	1.93
	62.60	90.68	23.36	37.15
mean rever is prof	60.31	61.62	93.35	74.24
mean rever hourly _is prof	60.03	54.42	95.57	69.36
rsi is prof	98.34	0.00	0.00	0.00
rsi hourly is prof	56.27	64.38	48.50	55.32
baseline is prof buy	92.09	55.21	10.66	17.88
sma is prof buy	91.53	0.00	0.00	0.00
sma hourly is prof buy	57.50	36.36	0.15	0.30
stoch is prof buy	56.83	33.00	3.91	7.00
stoch hourly is prof buy	53.34	42.67	30.06	35.27
mean rever is prof buy	66.04	66.42	93.41	77.64
mean rever hourly is prof	58.41	56.53	71.38	63.09
buy rsi is prof buy	98.36	0.00	0.00	0.00
rsi hourly is prof buy	43.18	59.43	5.31	9.75
best strategy sell	27.95	27.30	16.20	13.06
best strategy buy	12.68	15.73	13.50	8.65

with 27.95% accuracy. The best strategy just beat buy label baseline with baseline 12.68% accuracy, but did not beat the non hourly results in its similar result.

Table 11: XGB Hourly Results

The results for SVM hourly predictions can be seen in table 12. Again, all of the labels except rsi hourly is prof buy performed better than the random guessing baseline of 50%. The baseline is prof (sell), sma _is prof (sell), rsi is prof (sell) and rsi is prof buy labels had high accuracy values but 0 precision. The stoch hourly is prof (sell) had a high accuracy of 61.64% and high precision of 80.87%. The mean rever is prof buy, mean _ rever hourly is prof buy and stoch is prof buy also had high accuracies with reasonably high precision values. The best strategy buy and best strategy sell again beat baseline and the similar non hourly result.

Label	Accuracy	Precision	Recall	F1
baseline is prof	83.54	0.00	0.00	0.00
sma is prof sma hourly is prof	91.61	0.00	0.00	0.00
stoch is prof	54.17	41.27	0.92	1.81
stoch hourly is prof	61.98	48.98	2.05	3.94
	61.64	80.87	24.80	37.96
mean rever is prof	60.70	67.46	69.26	68.35
mean rever hourly _is prof	59.16	56.31	61.06	58.59
rsi is prof	98.34	0.00	0.00	0.00
rsi hourly is prof	56.82	63.35	53.74	58.15
baseline is prof buy	92.22	54.46	22.13	31.47
sma is prof buy	91.53	0.00	0.00	0.00
sma hourly is prof buy	57.55	0.00	0.00	0.00
stoch is prof buy	58.69	53.55	3.25	6.12
stoch hourly is prof buy	56.07	42.78	11.48	18.10
mean rever is prof buy	64.14	68.50	79.93	73.77
mean rever hourly is prof	58.67	57.02	69.07	62.47
buy rsi is prof buy	98.36	0.00	0.00	0.00
rsi hourly is prof buy	42.79	52.12	12.42	20.05
best strategy sell	29.85	20.36	15.98	12.39
best strategy buy	27.26	17.65	15.08	13.29

Table 12: SVM Hourly Results

Metric

Metric								
Accuracy	53.62	54.50	53.02	55.51	19.09	20.00	17.79	22.34
Precision	49.91	52.38	43.76	52.96	14.47	9.91	9.92	2.49
Recall	9.44	13.86	8.87	12.77	13.82	12.09	12.75	11.11

	Accuracy	Precision	Recall	F1
Label				
baseline is prof				
sma is prof sma				
hourly is prof				
stoch is prof				
stoch hourly is prof				
F1	14.81 20.18 13.35	19.30	11.15	7.68 8.93 4.06

Table 13: Averaged Results

The metrics of each model were averaged for the 'is profitable' labels and 'best strategy' labels to get an overview of the results. The per stock results can be seen

LR is profitable	RF is profitable	XGB is profitable	SVM is profitable	LR best -strategy	RF best strategy	XGB best strategy	SVM best strategy

in table 13. The most accurate model for the per stock data was SVM with an accuracy of 55.51% and precision of 52.96% on the binary classification labels. The best strategy was predicted with 22.34% accuracy.

The hourly results can be seen in table 14. The most accurate model for the hourly data was logistic regression with an accuracy of 69.93% and precision of 37.46%. The SVM classifier was not far behind logistic regression in terms of accuracy and slightly surpassed it in terms of precision. Random forest had the lowest accuracy but highest precision. The LR classifier performed best for predicting the best strategy for buying and selling with an

Metric	LR is profitable	RF is profitable	XGB is profitable	SVM is profitable	LR best -strategy	RF best strategy	XGB best strategy	SVM best strategy
Accuracy	69.93	67.02	69.03	69.33	29.54	26.58	20.32	28.56
Precision	37.46	40.82	39.61	38.15	16.82	17.79	21.52	19.01
Recall	26.39	20.26	28.73	22.78	15.30	14.46	14.85	15.53
F1	26.19	22.01	27.14	24.49	11.17	11.07	10.85	12.84

Table 14: Averaged Hourly Results

average accuracy of 29.54%.

5.1.1 Feature Importance

Feature importance plots were created for the most accurately predicted labels using the two best performing models. Figure 12 shows the feature importance plots resulting from using SVM on the per stock data. The 10 most important features for some of the accurately predicted labels were plotted. Feature importance for labels rsi is prof, sma is prof, stoch is prof, stoch hourly is prof and mean rever is prof are shown in these plots. Sector was the most important feature for predicting all of these labels. Industry was also important in predicting most of these labels. Returns and number of buys and sells for other labels were important to predicting these labels.

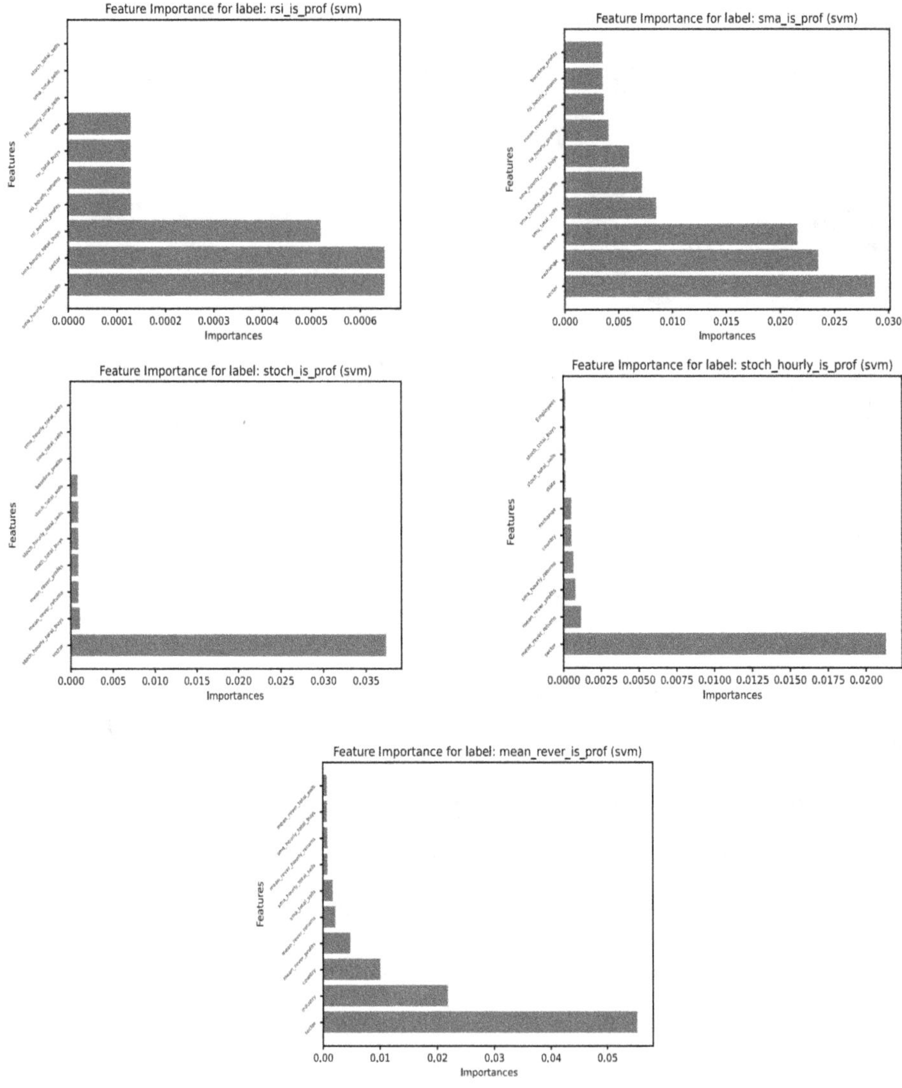

Figure 12: Feature Importance for SVM

Figure 13 shows the feature importance plots resulting from using logistic regression on the hourly data. The 10 most important features for some of the accurately predicted labels were plotted. Feature importance for labels baseline is _ prof buy, mean rever is prof buy, stoch is prof, stoch hourly is prof, mean rever is prof and mean rever hourly is prof are shown in these plots.

Hour was the most important feature for stoch hourly is prof, mean _rever is prof and
mean rever hourly is prof. The baseline _total buys feature was most important for predicting the stoch is prof label. Other important features for the label included mean rever hourly total buys, baseline total sells and sma hourly total _sells, rsi total buys and stoch hourly _total buys. The results of some strategies were important in predicting the success of other strategies. The hour itself was in the top 1 to 3 most important features for all of these labels except stoch is prof. This indicates that the hour itself is extremely important for predicting the success of trading strategies.

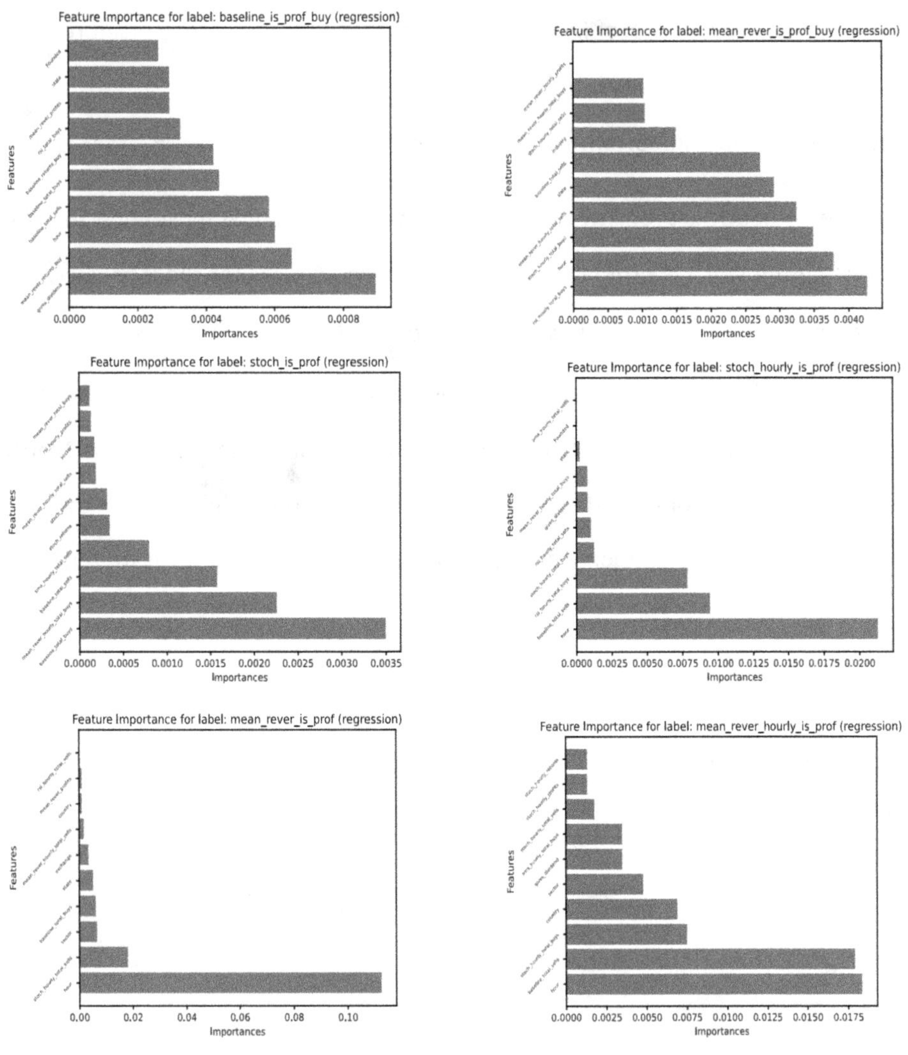

Figure 13: Feature Importance for Logistic Regression

5.2   Simulation Results

The successful strategies for each stock are presented in table 15 below. Successful strategies had account balances greater than $1000 after the trading period was complete.

symbol	strategy	total account value
AMAT	mean rever hourly	1019.43
AMAT	rsi	1271.49
AMAT	sma	1098.78
AMAT	sma hourly	1000.66
AMZN	meanrever	1000.58
AMZN	meanrever hourly	1018.48
AMZN	sma	1038.03
AMZN	sma hourly	1019.30
COST	baseline	1005.89
COST	meanrever	1001.45
COST	meanrever hourly	1001.30
COST	sma	1038.27
JNJ	sma	1036.56
JPM	sma	1014.47
JPM	stoch	1000.18
KO	rsi	1031.63
MSFT	sma	1068.15
ORCL	sma	1069.91
ORCL	sma hourly	1000.76
PEP	rsi	1067.06
TM	sma	1056.79
TSM	sma	1032.12
UNH	mean rever hourly	1007.57
WMT	mean rever	1000.34
WMT	mean rever hourly	1011.14
WMT	sma	1079.22

Table 15: Successful simulation strategies

The average gain per hour for successful hours and strategies are shown in table 16 below for TSLA and AMZN. Table 17 shows the average fain per hour due to buying at the specified hours.

symbol	strategy	hour	avg gain/loss	symbol	strategy	hour	avg gain/loss
TSLA	baseline	16	4.88	AMZN	baseline	16	2.30

TSLA sma 12 11.18 AMZN sma 9 19.02 TSLA sma 15 12.31 AMZN sma hourly 9 10.12 TSLA sma hourly 11 0.39 AMZN sma hourly 11 16.07

TSLA sma hourly 12 0.34 AMZN stoch 9 0.62 TSLA sma hourly 15 0.54 AMZN stoch 10 0.09 TSLA stoch 9 0.45 AMZN stoch 11 0.57 TSLA stoch 10 0.43 AMZN stoch hourly 9 0.52 TSLA stoch 14 0.08 AMZN stoch hourly 11 0.28 TSLA stochhourly 9 0.17 AMZN stoch hourly 12 0.09 TSLA stochhourly 11 0.33 AMZN stoch hourly 13 0.06

symbol	strategy	hour	avg gain/loss	symbol	strategy	hour	avg gain/loss
TSLA	stochhourly	12	0.52	AMZN	stoch hourly	14	0.17
TSLA	stochhourly	13	0.09	AMZN	stoch hourly	16	1.41

TSLA stochhourly 16 0.75 AMZN mean rever 9 1.01 TSLA mean rever 9 2.62 AMZN mean rever 10 0.52 TSLA mean rever 10 0.42 AMZN mean rever 11 0.137 TSLA mean rever 11 0.75 AMZN mean rever 12 0.36

symbol	strategy	hour	avg gain/loss	symbol	strategy	hour	avg gain/loss
TSLA	mean rever	12	0.68	AMZN	mean rever	13	0.44

TSLA mean rever 15 0.61 AMZN mean rever 14 0.26 TSLA mean reverhourly 9 9.40 AMZN mean rever 15 0.52 TSLA mean reverhourly 10 18.23 AMZN mean rever hourly 9 8.08 TSLA mean reverhourly 11 24.16 AMZN mean rever hourly 10 4.10

symbol	strategy	hour	avg gain/loss	symbol	strategy	hour	avg gain/loss
TSLA	mean reverhourly	13	6.64	AMZN	mean rever hourly	11	10.60
TSLA	mean reverhourly	14	10.89	AMZN	mean rever hourly	12	6.45

TSLA mean reverhourly 15 12.95 AMZN mean rever hourly 13 7.76 TSLA rsi hourly 9 27.48 AMZN mean rever hourly 14 2.45

symbol	strategy	hour	avg gain/loss	symbol	strategy	hour	avg gain/loss
TSLA	rsi hourly	11	3.20	AMZN	mean rever hourly	15	2.16

TSLA rsi hourly 13 2.61 AMZN rsi 9 86.39 TSLA rsi hourly 15 0.12 AMZN rsi hourly 9 10.22 TSLA rsi hourly 16 6.51 AMZN rsi hourly 12 1.42 AMZN rsi hourly 13 12.17

symbol	strategy	hour	avg gain/loss	symbol	strategy	hour	avg gain/loss
				AMZN	rsi hourly	16	5.30

Table 16: Successful simulation strategies - hourly

symbol	strategy	hour	gain/loss	symbol	strategy	hour	gain/loss
TSLA	baseline	9	4.88	AMZN	baseline	9	2.30
TSLA	sma	9	5.59	AMZN	sma	9	38.03

TSLA sma 15 12.31 AMZN sma hourly 9 32.46 TSLA sma hourly 11 1.53 AMZN sma hourly 16 20.23

TSLA sma hourly 12 0.23 AMZN stoch 9 0.46 TSLA sma hourly 13 0.21 AMZN stoch 10 0.41 TSLA stoch 9 1.01 AMZN stoch 15 0.23 TSLA stoch 11 2.06 AMZN stoch hourly 9 0.29 TSLA stoch 16 20.11 AMZN stoch hourly 9 0.29 TSLA stoch hourly 11 0.64 AMZN stoch hourly 10 0.13

symbol	strategy	hour	gain/loss	symbol	strategy	hour	gain/loss
TSLA	stoch hourly	15	0.41	AMZN	stoch hourly	11	0.28

Stock	Strategy	Period	Value	Stock	Strategy	Period	Value
TSLA	stoch hourly	16	6.37	AMZN	stoch hourly	12	0.06
TSLA	mean rever	9	0.54	AMZN	stoch hourly	13	0.12
TSLA	mean rever	10	1.11	AMZN	mean rever	9	1.28
TSLA	mean rever	11	0.83	AMZN	mean rever	10	0.22
TSLA	mean rever	12	0.82	AMZN	mean rever	11	0.38
TSLA	mean rever	13	0.39	AMZN	mean rever	12	0.44
TSLA	mean rever	14	0.92	AMZN	mean rever	14	1.02
TSLA	mean rever	16	15.40	AMZN	mean rever	15	0.29
TSLA	mean rever hourly	9	20.36	AMZN	mean rever hourly	9	4.88
TSLA	mean rever hourly	10	0.47	AMZN	mean rever hourly	10	5.87
TSLA	mean rever hourly	11	8.10	AMZN	mean rever hourly	11	10.29
TSLA	mean rever hourly	12	7.99	AMZN	mean rever hourly	12	10.17
TSLA	mean rever hourly	13	8.81	AMZN	mean rever hourly	14	8.38
TSLA	mean rever hourly	14	22.52	AMZN	mean rever hourly	15	2.14
TSLA	rsi hourly	10	1.12	AMZN	rsi	9	129.59
TSLA	rsi hourly	12	0.16	AMZN	rsi hourly	9	1.73
TSLA	rsi hourly	13	5.62	AMZN	rsi hourly	10	0.28
TSLA	rsi hourly	14	0.22	AMZN	rsi hourly	11	9.04
TSLA	rsi hourly	15	0.14	AMZN	rsi hourly	14	0.10
TSLA	rsi hourly	16	8.98	AMZN	rsi hourly	15	2.07
				AMZN	rsi hourly	16	9.35

Table 17: Successful simulation strategies when buying - hourly

The results from the ML models can be seen below. Table 18 shows the results using SVM for the per stock data. All labels performed better than baseline but mean rever is prof was the label with the highest accuracy and precision.

Label	Accuracy	Precision	Recall	F1
baseline is prof	67.61	73.56	85.07	78.90
sma is prof	57.62	26.56	29.36	27.89
sma hourly is prof	57.11	33.03	28.08	30.35
stoch is prof	55.57	51.80	32.39	39.86
stoch hourly is prof	50.83	0.00	0.00	0.00
mean rever is prof	77.08	77.08	100.00	87.06
mean rever hourly is prof	55.70	69.12	69.86	69.49
rsi is prof	55.06	0.00	0.00	0.00
rsi hourly is prof				

64.28 66.95 91.54 77.34 best strategy 29.58 22.16 13.23 11.73

Table 18: Per Stock Results

Table 19 shows the mean of the SVM results. The overall accuracy was 60.09% for the

is profitable labels and 29.58% for the best strategy labels.

Metric	svm is profitable	svm best strategy
Accuracy	60.09	29.58
Precision	44.23	22.16
Recall	48.48	13.23
F1	45.65	11.73

Table 19: Per Stock Averaged Results

Table 20 shows the results using logistic regression for the hourly data. Again, all labels beat baseline but the labels with the highest accuracy values and high precision included baseline is prof, baseline is prof buy, mean rever is prof.

Label	Accuracy	Precision	Recall	F1
baseline is prof	88.49	71.10	58.95	64.46
sma is prof	94.08	0.00	0.00	0.00
sma hourly is prof	52.37	41.90	13.06	19.91
stoch is prof	49.17	42.27	73.92	53.78
stoch hourly is prof	57.79	61.82	37.82	46.93
mean rever is prof	68.02	74.28	82.10	78.00
mean rever hourly _is prof	56.39	63.63	53.73	58.26
rsi is prof	94.19	0.00	0.00	0.00
rsi hourly is prof	58.07	58.27	89.11	70.46
baseline is prof buy	95.13	75.14	69.60	72.26

sma is prof buy	94.14	0.00	0.00	0.00
sma hourly is prof buy	55.86	50.62	23.72	32.30
stoch is prof buy	58.82	47.45	13.20	20.66
stoch hourly is prof buy	56.75	47.68	5.73	10.23
mean rever is prof buy	60.95	73.17	66.36	69.60
mean rever hourly is prof	53.97	64.40	36.83	46.86
buy rsi is prof buy	94.22	0.00	0.00	0.00
rsi hourly is prof buy	45.53	58.07	23.97	33.94
best strategy sell	34.70	18.70	23.99	19.78
best strategy buy	28.10	17.02	21.55	15.08

Table 20: Hourly Results

Table 21 shows the mean of the LR hourly results. The mean accuracy was 68.55% for the is profitable labels and 31.4% for the best _strategy labels. Both of these values beat their respective baselines.

Metric	regression is profitable	regression best strategy
Accuracy	68.55	31.40
Precision	46.10	17.86
Recall	36.01	22.77
F1	37.65	17.43

Table 21: Averaged Hourly Results

These machine learning results show that these predictive methods succeed in the subsequent time periods in addition to the initial time periods tested.

Table 22 shows two examples of predicted labels and actual results for the 18 stock symbols used in the simulation. The mean _rever is prof and mean _rever hourly is prof labels are shown for the per stock data. For the mean rever _is prof label all stocks had profitable predictions and only 5 were incorrect. For the mean rever hourly _is prof label 9 out of the 18 predictions were correct. The mean reversion and hourly mean reversion strategies were predicted to be profitable for AMZN over the time period. These predictions were correct as it can be seen in 15 that AMZN was profitable for both of those labels.

Stock Symbol	mean rever is prof	mean rever is prof prediction	mean rever hourly is prof	mean rever hourly is prof prediction
TSLA	1	1	1	1
TM	1	1	0	1
SBUX	0	1	0	1
AMZN	1	1	1	1
MSFT	1	1	1	0
ORCL	0	1	1	0
AMAT	1	1	1	0
TSM	1	1	1	1
MRNA	0	1	0	1
JNJ	0	1	0	1
WMT	1	1	1	1
COST	1	1	1	1
UNH	1	1	1	1
CVS	0	1	0	1
JPM	1	1	1	0
PYPL	1	1	1	1
PEP	1	1	1	1
KO	1	1	1	1

Table 22: Predictions

Table 23 shows one example of predicted labels and actual results for each hour of the day for two of the stocks. For TSLA 6 out of the 8 predictions were correct and for AMZN all of the predictions were correct. This table is just one small snapshot of all of the predictions.

Stock Symbol	Hour	mean -rever is -prof	mean rever is _ prof prediction
TSLA	9	1	1
TSLA	10	1	1
TSLA	11	1	1
TSLA	12	1	1
TSLA	1	0	1
TSLA	2	0	1
TSLA	3	1	1
TSLA	4	0	0
AMZN	9	1	1
AMZN	10	1	1
AMZN	11	1	1
AMZN	12	1	1

AMZN	1		1	1
AMZN	2		1	1
AMZN	3		0	0

Table 23: Predictions Hourly

These results show how predictions can be made regarding which trading strategies should be used for each stock. These predictions can be used to carry out a set of trades as was shown in the

simulation.

6 Discussion: Applications & Future Work

Our results show that we can reasonably predict if a specific trading strategy will be profitable or not over a 6 month period during each hour of the day. In practice this can be used in multiple ways.

One way to implement these results is by checking for buy and sell triggers for all trading strategy at every hour during a trading day. If different strategies suggest conflicting actions then the best predicted strategies for that hour can be prioritized.

Another way to use these results is if someone wants to start trading a certain stock on a specific day they can wait for the strategy that is most likely to be profitable for buying to trigger. When they want to sell they can wait for the signal most likely to be profitable when selling during that hour to trigger.

If someone is interested in using a specific trading strategy they can see if it is likely to be profitable during that time period. If it is and can be accurately predicted then it could be a good strategy to employ. If a strategy is predicted to be profitable with high accuracy it may be a good strategy to use. If a strategy is predicted to be not profitable for a given time period then that is also useful information and an investor may not want to trade based on that strategy triggering.

Like all trading strategies and indicators the ones presented here can be combined and adjusted based on specific needs. These results can be used as suggestions but still closely watched by the users. Other strategies can be used to create training data in the same way and predict if those strategies are likely to be profitable.

Some future steps include forward testing or testing the trading strategies on real-time live data. This could introduce other factors such as small price changes that may come with execution time. Testing our hypotheses on smaller or larger time blocks such as 15 minutes or 2 hours is another possible future step. Training data can be created using a different set of trading strategies and the same predictive methods can be applied. The feature set can also be updated to include more values or pared down to only focus on the features that proved to be most important.

7   Conclusion

While predicting stock market trends can be a challenging task, we showed that predicting the performance of stock strategies based on hour of the day for a given time period was more successful than predicting only on the overall time period. We also showed that the hour itself is a good predictor of how well a strategy will perform. The baseline value for predicting best strategies out of the nine options is 1/9 or 11.11% accuracy. The baseline value for predicting whether or not a strategy will be profitable over a given time period is 50%. The best strategy for a stock over a 6 month period was predicted with 22.34% accuracy, while predicting whether or not trading strategies would be successful was predicted with 55.51% accuracy. Both of these values beat their respective baselines. When looking at the data on an hourly basis the best strategy at a given hour over a 6 month period was predicted with 29.54% accuracy. Whether or not each trading strategy would be successful at each hour of the trading day was predicted with 69.93% accuracy. These values beat the non hourly predictions as well as their respective baselines. Rather than predicting stock price and direction we can predict which strategies are likely to succeed in a given time frame. This gives individual investors control and the ability to implement the strategies that work for them. This allows for flexibility where an investor can buy or sell at any hour of the day and get suggestions on which triggers are more likely to succeed later on. These results show that the hour of the day is related to, and in some cases influences, the trends in the stock market and that individual investors can capitalize on these movements on a daily and hourly basis.

Printed in the USA
CPSIA information can be obtained
at www.ICGtesting.com
CBHW061842091024
15572CB00017B/1444